The Palestinian Problem

and

United States Policy

To Bill + Lorna — w/ lots of love. Bruce + Liz

THE PALESTINIAN PROBLEM

AND

UNITED STATES POLICY

A Guide to Issues and References

Text by

BRUCE R. KUNIHOLM

Bibliographical Essay by

MICHAEL RUBNER

REGINA BOOKS
Claremont, California

Library of Congress Cataloging in Publication Data

Kuniholm, Bruce Robellet, 1942-
    The Palestinian problem and United States policy.

    (Guides to contemporary issues ; #5)
    Bibliography: p.
    1. Jewish-Arab relations - 1973 -   . 2. Palestinian Arabs--
Politics and Government. 3. West Bank--International Status.
4. Gaza Strip--International Status. 5. Jewish-Arab relations--1973-
--Bibliography. 6. United States--Foreign Relations--Israel--
Bibliography. 7. Israel--Foreign Relations--United States--
Bibliography. I. Rubner, Michael. II. Title. III. Series.
DS119.77.K86   016.3277305694   85-25687

ISBN 0-941690-18-0
ISBN 0-941690-19-9 pbk.

Regina Books
Box 280
Claremont, CA 91711
Manufactured in the United States of America

Guides to Contemporary Issues

Richard Dean Burns, Editor

This series is devoted to exploring contemporary social, political, economic, diplomatic and military issues. Each guide begins with an extended narrative which introduces opinions and interpretations regarding the issue under discussion, and concludes with a comprehensive bibliographical survey of the essential writings on the topic, including recent articles, books, and documents. The guides, consequently, are designed to provide reference librarians, academic researchers, students, and informed citizens with easy access to information concerning controversial issues.

This series has been developed, in part, in cooperation with the Center for the Study of Armament and Disarmament, California State University, Los Angeles.

#1 THE MX CONTROVERSY: A GUIDE TO ISSUES AND REFERENCES
Robert A. Hoover

#2 THE MILITARY IN THE DEVELOPMENT PROCESS
Nicole Ball

#3 THE PERSIAN GULF & UNITED STATES POLICY
Bruce R. Kuniholm

#4 CENTRAL AMERICA & UNITED STATES POLICIES, 1820s-1980s
Thomas M. Leonard

#5 THE PALESTINIAN PROBLEM & UNITED STATES POLICY
Bruce R. Kuniholm and Michael Rubner.

To

*Elizabeth, Jonathan and
Erin*

and

*Audrey, Daniel and
Jessica*

Foreword

This volume represents the unusual collaboration of two Middle Eastern specialists who, despite having never met, allowed me to preside over the merging of their contributions. Professor Bruce Kuniholm of Duke University initially suggested that the Palestinian issue deserved a critical reexamination. Subsequently, he developed the extended essay around which this book has been designed. This essay offers a coherent and thoughtful challenge to the conventional wisdom that has governed Palestinian-Israeli-American positions and that has held, generally, nothing can be done to resolve the outstanding issues.

With this essay in hand, I asked Professor Michæl Rubner of Michigan State University to search his extensive file of references to the Arab-Istræli conflict for some 500 books and articles which could allow a researcher to explore further the points raised in Kuniholm's essay. Professor Rubner's prompt response more than fulfilled my most optimistic expectations. He not only provided the desired selections, but proceeded in essay fashion to introduce various political, economic and military issues and to indentify those books and articles carrying a Palestinian, Israeli, or American view.

The professionalism and collegiality of these two scholars has resulted, consequently, in a challenging study of one of the Middle East's most preplexing dilemmas. Policymakers, students and laymen should find Kuniholm's questions and analysis stimulating, and scholars and librarians will find Rubner's bibliographical essay an invaluable guide to the general literature.

Richard Dean Burns
Series Editor

Contents

PART ONE

ANALYSIS

by

Bruce R. Kuniholm

Introduction

The Palestinian problem derives from conflicting Palestinian and Isræli claims to Palestine. In its present form, the problem is essentially a clash between Isræl's search for security and the Palestinian quest for self-determination. Meron Benvenisti, the former Deputy Mayor of Jerusalem, has emphasized the "zero-sum" nature of the conflict—"the perception, equally shared by both Isrælis and Arabs, that what one side can win equals what the other side must lose"—and has argued that third parties have underestimated difficulties associated with its resolution. Nevertheless, numerous administrations in the United States have asserted that the conflict is *not* a zero-sum game, that a mutually beneficial compromise is possible, and that a Palestinian entity in the territories now occupied by Isræl could be in the interests not only of the Palestinians, but also of both Isræl and the United States. Clearly, much would depend on the structure of the process by which such an entity were to evolve, the guarantees that Isræl would receive, and the overall context within which these developments would take place. History may offer scant hope for melioration of the problem, but the imperatives that drive U.S. foreign policy demand that means be found to mediate and, if possible, reconcile the conflict between Arab and Jew. Even if reconciliation seems impossible, these imperatives suggest that an effort must nonetheless be made.[1]

---

[1]Meron Benvenisti, *Jerusalem: Study of a Polarized Community* (Jerusalem: West Bank Data Base Project, 1983), p. 121.

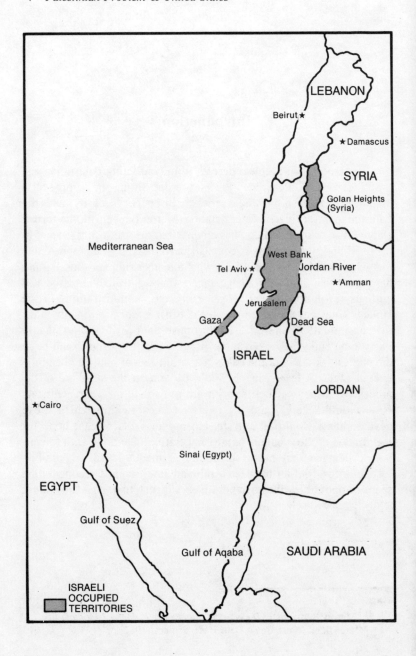

LEBANON

Beirut ★

★ Damascus

SYRIA

Golan Heights
(Syria)

Mediterranean Sea

West Bank

Jordan River

Tel Aviv ★

★ Amman

Jerusalem

Gaza

Dead Sea

ISRAEL

JORDAN

★ Cairo

Sinai (Egypt)

EGYPT

Gulf of Suez

Gulf of Aqaba

SAUDI ARABIA

ISRAELI
OCCUPIED
TERRITORIES

I

THE QUESTION OF PALESTINIAN SELF-DETERMINATION

This monograph examines the Palestinian problem and discusses its implications for U.S. policy. As a means to this end, arguments for and against Palestinian self-determination are considered in some detail. Since self-determination, unqualified by anything other than normal constraints, would lead to the establishment of a state for the Palestinians, the question of a Palestinian state will also be examined.

A Palestinian state, it should be clearly noted, is not a solution that the U.S. government supports. Most Palestinians may insist on it, but the Isrælis totally reject the notion, while the plan proposed by the Reagan administration in September 1982 also opposes it. What the Reagan Plan proposes (and what President Carter also favored) is a compromise between Palestinian and Isrælli desires—Palestinian self-government in association with Jordan.[2]

The extent to which the Palestinians should have self-government in the West Bank and Gaza—whether or not in association with Jordan—causes serious controversy in all deliberations over the requirements for a comprehensive settlement of the Arab-Isrælli conflict. This is as true of debates within the Palestine National Council (P.N.C.), the *de facto* Palestinian parliament, as it is of debates within the World Zionist Congress and Isræl. The reason for such controversy is that, more than any issue, the question of Palestinian self-

---

[2]For Carter's perference that the Palestinians have a homeland tied to Jordan or a larger confederation, see Cyrus Vance, *Hard Choices: Critical Years in America's Foreign Policy* (New York: Simon & Schuster, 1983), p. 177.

government raises the question of entitlement to the West Bank and Gaza, which in turn lays bare the psychological and emotional factors that are at the root of the conflict. These factors explain why both the Palestinian leadership and the Israeli government until recently have rejected the Reagan administration's attempt to address their concerns and, to some extent, they corroborate the judgment of those who see the Arab-Israeli conflict as a zero-sum game.

In view of these profound differences, the question of whether or not the Palestinians can or should determine their own future in the West Bank and Gaza strip serves as a convenient framework for discussing the Palestinian problem. Presented in stark terms, the question may be somewhat artificial in the sense that whatever the outcome, the result will have to be a compromise of sorts; neither self-determination for the Palestinians nor its denial by Israel will be without qualification. Arguments for and against self-determination are not necessarily mutually exclusive; they are often subject to qualification and compromise, and are complicated by related arguments which may on occasion be usefully separated from them. Arguments in favor of Israeli withdrawal from the occupied territories, for example, do not *ipso facto* suggest the conclusion that those territories ought to be controlled, either exclusively or at all, by the Palestinians. One could argue (as the Reagan administration does) that they should be turned over to the Jordanians or (as some Israelis assert) to a joint Israeli-Jordanian condominium. Nevertheless, approaching the question from two general points of view helps to focus the debate between the Israelis and Palestinians and allows for a relatively clear exposition of their primary concerns.

Our focus will remain on the Palestinian problem. We want in particular to avoid being distracted by the latest complications over the prolonged war in Lebanon. The Israeli invasion of Lebanon, we must keep in mind, was precipitated by the Palestinian problem, and Lebanon's future will depend as much on satisfactory resolution of that problem as it will on the accommodation of external powers or reform of the Lebanese political system. The intention here is to provide those individuals concerned about the broader questions of U.S. policy with some insight into the Palestinian context of the Arab-Israeli question, to illuminate the fundamental problems that continue to separate so many Palestinians and Israelis, and to illustrate why certain concerns affect their differing perceptions of President Reagan's peace initiative of

September 1, 1982. Then, after examining the manner in which the United States became involved in the Palestinian question, and the moral implications of that involvement, our concern is to shed light on the U.S. stake in attempting to resolve the Palestinian question, to provide a sense of the gaps that will have to be bridged if a settlement is ever to be achieved, and to explore how the United States might encourage the process.

Arguments Supporting Palestinian Self-Determination

The line of reasoning leading to the conclusion that the Palestinians need a state of their own begins with the premise that the creation of a Palestinian state (which the Palestinians want and which would be consistent with their legitimate right to self-determination) would rectify previous injustices and restore Palestinian dignity. The Egyptians understand the importance of this psychological process. What made it possible for President Sadat to travel to Jerusalem in 1977 was the fact that Egypt's humiliating defeat of 1967 had been erased in 1973.

The Isrælis, too, should understand the importance of this process. The trial of Adolf Eichmann served as a first opportunity for many Isrælis to face their past squarely. According to Amos Elon, the Eichmann verdict played a role in preparing the ground emotionally for the resumption of normal relations with all things German. If Isræl, with the help of the United States, addresses legitimate grievances and develops a fair solution to Palestinian problems, the Palestinians may finally come to terms with the Isrælis.[3]

The 1982 war in Lebanon, which included the massacre of hundreds of Palestinians by Christian Phalangist militiamen, and for which the Isrælis bear indirect responsibility, has underscored the Palestinians' need for a home of their own. Like the Jews before them, the Palestinians in their diaspora have been forced to conclude that only self-rule in a state of their own can assure them control over their own

---

[3] Amos Elon, *The Isrælis: Founders and Sons* (New York: Bantam, 1971, 1972), p. 280.

lives. This is a lesson they have learned not from the Isrælis but from their fellow Arabs: the Jordanians who crushed them in 1970-1971; the Syrians who turned on them in 1975-1976; Lebanon's Christian Maronites who, as noted above, massacred them at Sabra and Shatila in 1982; the Syrians once again, who ousted them from Tripoli in 1983; and most recently Lebanon's Shiite Muslim militia, Amal, which with Syrian assistance conducted a month-long siege on three Palestinian refugee camps (including Sabra and Shatila) in 1985, killing hundreds.

Like Isrælis and Jews all over the world, Palestinians identify with the land of Palestine. Palestinians lived on the land for centuries. Before being ousted and fleeing from a part of war-torn Palestine in 1948, Palestinians owned most of the land and constituted two-thirds of the population. Since then, Palestinians have lived under Jordanian, Egyptian, and Isræli rule, and in exile. Isræl has granted citizenship to Palestinians in Isræl, but has given them unequal treatment. Arab countries, except for Jordan, have not offered the mass of Palestinian refugees citizenship (there have been relatively rare exceptions), nor have the Palestinian desired assimilation. They prefer instead to maintain a separate identity, based on ties to the land from which they came and maintained by a developing sense of themselves as a nation-in-exile. A Palestinian state, which is consistent (as Isræli sovereignty over the occupied territories is not) with U.N. Security Council Resolution 242 (1967), and which is consonant with the ideal of self-determination embodied in the United Nations Charter, would meet their needs and fulfill their dreams.[4]

---

[4]Those who seek to legitimate the Palestinian cause argue that the Palestinians deserved the right to independence after World War I. Among the factors contributing to this judgment are President Woodrow Wilson's espousal of autonomous development for nationalities under Ottoman rule in his 14 Points; the agreement in 1915 between the Emir Hussein, Sherif of Mecca, and Sir Henry McMahon, the British High Commissioner in Egypt, which under one reasonable interpretation promised independence to the Arabs in Palestine; and the Arab Revolt against the Turks in 1916, which fulfilled the terms of the agreement. Instead, against the wishes of the population (as evidenced by the findings of the King-Crane Commission), the British Mandate ignored the right of the

Most Palestinians—particularly those who live in the occupied territories—recognize that they cannot recover all of Palestine. What they seek is that part in which many still live: the West Bank, East Jerusalem, and Gaza. A state formed from these territories, many believe, need not be a place of residence for all Palestinians. Some, under U.N. General Assembly Resolution 194 III (1948), would seek compensation for their property rather than return. For others, the main issue is attainment of a political identity. But a Palestinian's right to return, most argue, must be no less than that accorded Jews under Israel's Law of Return, which provides every Jew a right to immigrate to Israel. Absorption, they believe, if it is a problem, should be one for the Palestinians to solve.[5]

Arabs in Palestine to self-determination and imposed upon them a pro-Zionist solution that could only be carried out by force of arms. See George Antonius, *The Arab Awakening: The Story of the Arab National Movement* (New York: Capricorn, 1946, 1965), pp. 164-183, 413-427, 443-458. During the course of the mandate, others argue, an important part of the Balfour Declaration was disregarded (i.e., the clause noting the clear understanding "that nothing shall be done which may prejudice the civil and religious rights of existing non-Jewish communities in Palestine"). The 1947 decision by the U.N. to partition Palestine continued the history of bias against the Palestinians; it was reflected not only in how the boundary lines were drawn (56 per cent of the land went to one third of the population, which only owned 6 per cent of it) but in who voted for and against partition (i.e., former colonial powers and their friends against emerging third world countries). See Fawzi Asadi, "Some Geographic Elements in the Arab-Israeli Conflict," *Journal of Palestine Studies* 6 (Autumn 1976), pp. 79-91.

[5]As a Palestinian author has written, "Palestine is no longer a mere geographical entity, but a state of mind. The reason, however, that Palestinians are obsessed with the notion of Return, though indeed there is no Palestine to return to as it was a quarter of a century before, is because the Return means the reconstitution of a Palestinian's integrity and the regaining of his place in history. It is not merely for a physical return to Palestine that a lot of men and women have given or dedicated

Walid Khalidi, a prominent Palestinian scholar and member of the Palestine National Council, declares that only a Palestinian state is likely to effect a psychological breakthrough for the Palestinians under occupation and in the diaspora. This explains the Palestine Liberation Organization (P.L.O.) condemnation of the September 1982 Reagan initiative.[6] President Reagan's opposition to an independent Palestinian state meant that he rejected what the Palestinians regard as their inalienable right to self-determination. Instead, the United States continued to ask the Palestinians to recognize Israel without a *quid pro quo* (i.e., Israeli recognition of Palestinian national rights). Sabri Jiryis, an Israeli-Arab lawyer who subsequently became Director of the P.L.O. Research Center in Beirut before it was destroyed in the 1982 war, has observed that "Recognition, like marriage, must be mutual." It should be the task of the United States to facilitate mutual recognition of national rights, the Palestinians would argue, because peace is possible only on the basis of mutual respect and dignity.[7]

----

their lives, but for the right to return of which they have been robbed." Fawaz Turki, *The Disinherited: Journal of a Palestinian Exile*, 2nd ed. (New York: Monthly Review Press, 1972, 1974), pp. 175-76. Internationally, the acceptance of a Palestinian identity is relatively recent. The Balfour Declaration (1917) refers to Palestinians (then 90 per cent of the population) as one of the "existing non-Jewish communities," while U.N. Security Council Resolution 242 (1967) refers to Palestinians as "the refugee problem." For elaboration of the argument that the Palestinians have a legal right to self-determination under international law, see W. Thomas Mallison and Sally V. Mallison, "The National Rights of the People of Palestine," *Journal of Palestine Studies* 9 (Summer 1980), pp. 119-130.

[6]Walid Khalidi, "Thinking the Unthinkable: A Sovereign Palestinian State," *Foreign Affairs* 56 (July 1978), pp. 695-713.

[7]Sabri Jiryis, "On Political Settlement in the Middle East: The Palestinian Dimension," *Journal of Palestine Studies* 7 (Autumn 1977), pp. 3-25. For a reiteration of this formula in November 1982 by Khalid Hassan, chairman of the foreign relations committee of the Palestine National Council, see the *Christian*

If mutual recognition leads to the establishment of a Palestinian state, many of the factors that now fuel Arab hostility and Palestinian irredentism could be diminished. The Fez Summit's call for an independent Palestinian state in September 1982 indicated that the Arab world (with few exceptions such as Libya or the People's Democratic Republic of Yemen) would endorse a solution acceptable to a majority of Palestinians. Solutions short of a Palestinian state, of course, are more problematic. The Casablanca Summit's failure to endorse a confederated Jordanian-Palestinian state in August 1985 also suggests that Syria's role is crucial; as long as President Hafez al-Assad is in power his interests (which will be discussed later) must be addressed. Should that difficult condition be met, general Arab support even for a confederated state would probably follow. In any event, whatever form it takes, a Palestinian government operating out of the West Bank and Gaza, and under the control of nationalists who predominate in both the Palestine National Council and (even after the rebellion within its ranks) in the Fatah wing of the P.L.O., would probably be anxious to respect Israeli sovereignty and would be sufficiently cohesive (given Syria's stake in its success) to prevent terrorist attacks by ideologues and extremist groups. Why? To avoid the consequences of Israeli retaliation. Palestinians would now have something to lose, something for which they themselves would be responsible. A port on the Mediterranean would serve the same function (i.e., a hostage to fortune) that the city of Suez served on the Gulf of Suez in the rapprochement between Israel and Egypt.

Daily interaction between Israelis and Palestinians (approximately half of the West Bank's labor force now works in Israel) provides a

---

Science Monitor, Nov. 4, 1982. Hassan believed that Israel would not recognize the P.L.O. even if the P.L.O. recognized Israel's right to exist, and that this is why the United States wanted Jordan to negotiate for the Palestinians. At present, the United States will not talk with the P.L.O. unless it accepts U.N. Resolutions 242 and 338 and recognizes Israel's right to exist (conditions that were stipulated in 1975 in an agreement between Israel and the United States). See Philip Geyelin, *Washington Post*, May 8, 1985, and the letter in the *Post*, May 25, 1985, by Mel Levine. The problems this policy poses for moderate Palestinians continue to be stumbling blocks in 1985.

reason to believe that, if the Palestinians are given the opportunity to be responsible for their own fate, mutually beneficial economic interaction would continue and even improve.[8] Brian Van Arkadie, who undertook a study of the West Bank and Gaza economies for the Carnegie Endowment, argues that the territories could benefit from wider leeway to define and pursue their own economic self-interest.[9]

Some who disagree with Van Arkadie have argued that Israeli withdrawal from the territories might culminate in Israeli producers losing access to West Bank/Gaza markets, and that Israel might lose the services of the 70,000 migrant Palestinians from the territories who now constitute about one-third of Israel's agricultural and industrial low-skilled labor. The counter argument, however, is that while disruptive in the short-term, such economic losses, even if they were to occur, would not be intolerable, particularly because the territories now import less than 12 per cent of Israel's output and because jobs held by migrant Palestinian labor might be taken over by Israeli Arabs. Whatever the case, the issue of "economic viability" may be irrelevant. Israel would not be economically viable without U.S. aid, while the "moderates" in the Arab world, led by Saudi Arabia, could provide financial support sufficient to ensure the viability of a Palestinian state and thereby limit Soviet influence over it. Furthermore, the inter-dependence between the

---

[8] Meron Benvenisti points out that officially 39,000 (29 per cent) out of 131,000 West Bank Palestinians are employed in Israel, but that 20,000 are unofficially employed and 15,000 are employed in local West Bank enterprises that serve as Israeli subcontractors. Meron Benvenisti, The West Bank and Gaza Data Base Project, *Interim Report* No. 1 (Jerusalem: The West Bank Data Base Project, 1982), p.5. According to Trudy Rubin, 38,000 Palestinian laborers commute daily to fields, factories, and construction sites in Israel., see *Christian Science Monitor*, Aug. 16, 1983.

[9] Brian Van Arkadie, *Benefits and Burdens: Report on the West Bank and Gaza Strip Economies Since 1967* (New York: Carnegie Endowment for International Peace, 1977), p. 154; Vivian Bull, *The West Bank—Is It Viable?* (Lexington, Mass.: D.C. Heath, 1975); and Elias Tuma, "The Economic Viability of a Palestinian State," *Journal of Palestine Studies* 7 (Spring 1978), pp. 102-124.

economies of Israel, Jordan, and a Palestinian state could serve as a foundation for a "common market" economy. With over 50,000 university graduates and thousands of civil servants employed through out the Arab world, the Palestinian manpower pool is better educated and more capable than that of most countries of the Third World. In addition, the West Bank already has an indigenous political system with viable social, administrative, political, and institutional infrastructures that could serve as a nucleus for a national entity.[10]

Some prospect for resolution of the problem of Jerusalem is essential for progress to be made on a political settlement. Palestinians regard access to the city as crucial because of its symbolic, emotional, political, and economic significance. Walid Khalidi asserts that "Without East Jerusalem, there would be no Palestinian state."[11] A number of analysts have examined imaginative alternatives for the resolution of conflicting Palestinian and Israeli positions on Jerusalem. While no one denies the difficulty of this issue, and most agree that it should not be dealt with at the outset of discussions, many believe that a solution is workable in the context of a comprehensive agreement on other issues. Their judgments are based on the feasibility of inventive formulæ that establish a borough system or create two municipalities which circumvent thorny debates over territorial rights. While not without problems, such proposals suggest that the positions of Israelis and Palestinians are not irreconcilable and that this most difficult of all problems need not preclude the establishment of a Palestinian state nor prevent an overall settlement of the Arab-Israeli conflict.[12]

---

[10]Emile Nakhleh, *The West Bank and Gaza: Towards the Making of a Palestinian State* (Washington, D.C.: American Enterprise Institute, 1974), p. 65. John Cooley, *Green March, Black September: The Story of the Palestinian Arabs* (London: Frank Cass, 1973), p. 69, puts the number of university graduates at 50,000.

[11]Khalidi, "Thinking the Unthinkable," p. 705.

[12]Evan Wilson, *Jerusalem: Key to Peace* (Washington, D.C.: Middle East Institute, 1970); Eugene Bovis, *The Jerusalem Question* (Stanford: Hoover Institution Press, 1971); Meron Benvenisti, *Jerusalem, the Torn City* (Minneapolis: University of Minnesota Press, 1976); and Benvenisti, *Jerusalem: Study of a Polarized Community*, cited earlier.

On the important issue of security, Israel will always have a crucial deterrent: the power to crush the Palestinians should punitive action be required. If a Palestinian state were to be established, Israel obviously would have a difficult time deciding which hostile actions warranted various levels of punitive responses. It would have to develop a sophisticated concept of deterrence. Such a problem is not insurmountable. The legitimacy and recognition accorded the Palestinian state, meanwhile, could foster the goodwill and predictable behavior necessary for peace. According to Major General Mattityahu Peled, former member of the Israeli General Staff in 1967, any knowledgeable Israeli who argues for keeping the occupied territories on security grounds is consciously lying. A Palestinian state, he asserts, would provide Israel with far greater security than possession of that same territory ever could. Peled's opinion, however, is not representative of Israeli judgments.[13]

Another means of approaching the security question is through American guarantees, which could compensate for the loss of strategic depth and reinforce Israel's deterrent posture. Those guarantees could be made more credible by an Israeli stake in the NATO alliance (air bases, prepositioned project stocks, land-based forces, and a role in defending strategic maritime areas in the eastern Mediterranean) which could establish the principle of interdependence between the United States and Israel.[14] In addition, security threats to Israel could be diminished by the broader context of a comprehensive Palestinian settlement. The Japanese and Austrian peace treaties after World War II contain useful precedents in that those countries chose to accept constitutional

---

[13]"Israel on the Edge of Elections: An Israeli General and Two Palestinian Mayors Talk About the Future," *Village Voice*, May 27-June 2, 1981; a variation of this idea was expressed by King Hussein to Secretary Vance: "Security is less a matter of geography and borders than a state of mind and a feeling of wanting to live in peace." See Vance, *Hard Choices*, p. 176.

[14]For discussion of this issue, see Shai Feldman, "Peacemaking in the Middle East: The Next Step," *Foreign Affairs* 60 (Spring 1981), pp. 756-780.

restraints on their military capabilities and their conduct of foreign policy, respectively. The Palestinians could do the same.

Many of the arguments for a Palestinian state being in Israel's best interests flow from the fact of Israel's limited resources. Israel's enormous defense expenditures, which account for nearly 30 per cent of its national income (G.N.P.), have contributed to triple-digit inflation since 1979 (117 per cent for 1981, 131.5 per cent for 1982, 190.7 per cent for 1983, and 444.7 per cent for 1984). Such rates cannot be sustained indefinitely.[15] Israeli trade deficits ($5.1 billion in 1983 and $5.2 billion in 1984) have also been problematic, while Israel's foreign debt of $24.4 billion is, in per capita terms, the largest in the world. According to one recent estimate, approximately 35 per cent of the budget is required to service the national debt.[16] Clearly, while peace would be expensive, continued hostility between Arab and Jew will cause an even greater long-term drain on Israel's resources, affecting not only the economy but, because of the trials of being an occupying force, the very psyche and identity of the nation. A Palestinian state, on the other hand, offers the possibility of true peace, a decreasing defense budget, a viable economy, and ultimately prosperity for both Arab and Jew.

Current demographic trends do not bode well for Israel's long-run viability as a Jewish state if it continues to hold on to the occupied territories.[17] These trends include a declining Jewish immigration (less

---

[15]See Samih Farsoun, "Begin's Distractionism," in *New York Times*, Aug. 2, 1982; *International Herald Tribune*, Aug. 11, 1983; *Jerusalem Post* (International Edition), Nov. 17, 1984; and *CRS Issue Brief* IB85066 (Updated 04/30/85).

[16]See Bernard Avishai, "The Victory of the New Israel," *New York Review of Books*, Aug. 13, 1981; Trudy Rubin, *Christian Science Monitor*, Aug. 26, 1983; and *CRS Issue Brief* IB84138 (Updated 04/30/85), Table IV.

[17]Samih Farsoun, *New York Times*, Aug. 2, 1982; see Dwight Simpson, "Israel After Thirty Years," *Current History* 76 (Jan. 1979). Arthur Hertzberg more recently has argued that this demographic argument is probably not true. The high rate of emigration from the West Bank, according to Hertzberg, means that the high birth rate in the region does not dictate a growth

than 11,000 in 1981), an increasing emigration (20,000 in 1981), and the wide disparity between Arab and Jewish birth rates in Isræl (Isræli Arabs have a growth rate of 3.5 per cent, double the 1.8 per cent growth rate of Isræli Jews).[18] Together these trends suggest that the 700,000

---

in the Arab population. Hertzberg, "Isræl and the West Bank: The Implications of Permanent Control," *Foreign Affairs* 61 (Summer 1983), pp. 1064-1077. These statistics are borne out to some extent by Benvenisti, who notes that the average annual growth rate of the population of the West Bank between 1968 and 1980 was 1.4 per cent, that of the population of Isræl 2.53 per cent, and that of the non-Jewish population of Isræl 3.93 per cent. The West Bank and Gaza Data Base Project, Interim Report No. 1; Uziel Schmelz of the Isræli Bureau of Statistics, however, has observed that in 1982 net emigration from the West Bank dropped by half in comparison with recent years because of the slide in the oil economy of the Gulf and the greater political problems for the Palestinians in their diaspora. Trudy Rubin, *Christian Science Monitor*, Aug. 16, 1983.

[18] According to sources cited by Arthur Hertzberg, former Defense Minister Ariel Sharon hoped the Lebanese War would start a flight of Palestinians to the eastern borders and, eventually, to Jordan. Hertzberg, "The Tragedy and the Hope," *New York Review of Books*, Oct. 21, 1982. Joseph Harsch in the *Christian Science Monitor*, Nov. 9, 1982, also notes that the Isrælis "are frank about their intention to push most of the Arabs out of the West Bank and Gaza into Jordan." Palestinians, needless to say, are not assured by off-hand remarks such as deputy Knesset speaker Meir Cohen's comment that present troubles could have been avoided if 200,000 to 300,000 Palestinians had been driven from the West Bank in 1967 as they had been expelled in 1948. Fears of being forced to leave were heightened by violence in Hebron in the summer of 1983. Cohen, *Christian Science Monitor*, Aug. 16, 1983. See also Jonathan Kuttab, "Palestinians see Expulsion Coming," *International Herald Tribune*, Aug. 4, 1983. For similar concerns in Lebanon, where the Lebanese government desired to evict as many as 300,000 Palestinians, see Bernard Gwertzman, *International Herald Tribune*, Aug. 18, 1983. In light of events, it seems clear that Fouad Ajami's assessment is correct: "The war in Lebanon was a war for the West Bank." Ajami, "The Shadows of Hell," *Foreign Policy* 48 (Fall 1982), pp. 94-110.

or so Arabs living in Israel (a figure that does not include the occupied territories) will continue to increase relative to the approximately three million Jews who live there (an additional 500,000 Israeli Jews live outside of Israel). If Israel retains control of the West Bank and Gaza (with a combined population of 1,240,000 Palestinians) over the next two or three decades, and demographic trends of the last decade continue, Jews could constitute a *minority* in Israel and the occupied territories— *unless* Israel chooses to step up repressive policies to drive the Palestinians out.

If Israel persists in rejecting Palestinian self-determination, whether by repression or eviction, the foundations of Israeli society can only be eroded by the resulting hostility. According to a comprehensive study of Israel's methods of control over its minority Arab population, these policies will have to become more repressive if control is to be maintained. Repression is certainly characteristic of Israeli policies toward the Arabs in the occupied territories. Confiscation of land for the establishment of new Israeli settlements, control of West Bank water resources, closure of Palestinian universities, censorship of library materials, dismissal and deportation of freely elected officials, prohibition of political assembly, detention of individuals without trial or explanation, curtailment of financial support for municipal services and development, and promotion of the so-called "village leagues" (armed and financed by the Israelis in spite of rejection by every well-known West Bank figure), all are part of a policy that increasingly alienates the Palestinian Arabs—the vast majority of whom continue to

---

This opinion is echoed by former Assistant Secretary of State Harold Saunders, who argues that the Israeli invasion "was designed to destroy once and for all any hope among the people of the West Bank and Gaza that the process of shaping the Palestinian people into a nation could succeed. It was designed to break any final resistance to total Israeli control...." Harold Saunders, "An Israeli-Palestinian Peace," *Foreign Affairs* 61 (Fall 1982), pp. 100-121. For the American role in the invasion, see Zeev Schiff, "Green Light, Lebanon," *Foreign Policy* 50 (Spring 1983), pp. 73-85. Ironically, the Israeli ambassador to London Shlomo Argov, whose shooting was used as a pretext for the invasion, has charged that the "senseless" adventure has weakened Israel. *Christian Science Monitor*, July 11, 1983.

support the moderate factions of the Palestine Liberation Organization.[19] Alienation is likely to be even more severe if, like the Algerian resistance to the French in the 1960s, Shiite resistance to the Isræli occupation of southern Lebanon in the 1980s is regarded as a militant example to be emulated.

Isræli policies toward the Palestinians will also create difficulties for Isræl's Jewish citizens who value the humanistic traditions of Judaism. Avraham Ahituv, who formerly headed the Shin Bet (the Isræli equivalent of the FBI), in August 1983 publicly charged that Isræl's settlements encouraged lawlessness and served as a psychological hothouse for the growth of Jewish terrorism. Settlers, he argued, have learned that illegal activities are sanctioned because the Likud government is politically sympathetic to their aims. His argument was borne out in July 1985 following the conviction of 15 Jews for shooting and killing Arab students at an Islamic college, planting explosives in mosques and on buses, and plotting to blow up the Dome of the Rock in Jerusalem, the third holiest Muslim shrine. Lawyers representing the convicted men insisted that the proper label for them was "patriot," not "terrorist," while Foreign Minister Yitzhak Shamir (formerly on the high command of Lohamey Heruth Isræl, known to many as the terrorist "Stern Gang"), described them as "boys who had erred," and vowed to work for their early release. Less extremist Isrælis, according to Jonathan Kuttab, a Palestinian lawyer who is the director of a human rights office in the West Bank, are being inured to violence by a dehumanization of Palestinians (e.g., references by public officials to "two-legged animals" and "drugged cock roaches

---

[19]Ian Lustick, *Arabs in a Jewish State: Isræl's Control over a National Minority* (Austin: University of Texas Press, 1980), pp. 266-271; see also Bernard Avishai, "Do Isræl's Arabs Have a Future?" *New York Review of Books*, Feb. 19, 1981. Former Foreign Minister Abba Eban has observed that Isræl's internal structure would not permit mass deportation and that it would create revulsion in Isræl. Trudy Rubin, *Christian Science Monitor*, Aug. 16, 1983. For moderate support for Arafat, see Jonathan Randal, *Washington Post*, Jan. 17, 1985, and a written text handed to Assistant Secretary of State Murphy in Jerusalem on Apr. 16, 1985, by 38 Palestinian leaders, reprinted in *Palestine Perspectives* 16 (May 1985), p. 7.

in a bottle"). In an essay styled as a eulogy for the humanistic tradition in Israel and a plea for a new beginning, Meron Benvenisti has observed that the prospect of ruling over more than a million Arabs without full democratic rights raises serious concerns about Israel being either Jewish or democratic. It also raises the profound question of whether the entire Zionist conception can be made to fit the situation that is developing in Israel and the occupied territories.[20]

Israel, it can be argued, is progressively losing control over its own fate, and not just because of the erosion of its humanistic traditions. As a result of its limited financial resources and the vast defense expenditures, Israel's foreign debt was $24.4 billion at the end of 1984, and rising steadily. In 1985 it will cost Israel $4.265 billion to service its foreign debt (with over $1 billion in interest going to the United States, to which Israel owes $10.235 billion). Foreign aid generates approximately half of Israel's GNP, and 75 to 80 per cent of that aid, if one counts all means of support, comes from the United States. Economic and military assistance from Washington (not including private transfers, economic infrastructural support, contingency economic support, or concessional aid) has fluctuated since the Camp David Accords between a high of $4.9 and a low of $1.8 billion a year. This amount, former Undersecretary of State George Ball pointed out, equals roughly $3,500 to $4,000 per year for every family of five in Israel. Recent trends, moreover, suggest that this dependency will increase. The amount of U.S. aid to Israel in FY 1985 was $2.6 billion—all in outright grants. In 1985 a supplemental economic grant of $1.5 billion (to be split between FY 1985 and FY 1986) was pending

---

[20]Ann Mosely Lesch, *Political Perceptions of the Palestinians on the West Bank and Gaza Strip* (Washington, D.C.: Middle East Institute, 1980); for more recent evidence of West Bank support for Arafat, see Trudy Rubin, *Christian Science Monitor*, July 1, 1983; David Ottoway, *International Herald Tribune*, July 13, 1983; Edward Walsh, *Washington Post*; Aug. 24, 1983; Trudy Rubin, *Christian Science Monitor*, Aug. 25, 1983; Meron Benvinisti, "The Turning Point," *New York Review of Books*, Oct. 13, 1983, pp. 11-16, and the sources cited in fn. 24. For a running chronicle of Israeli policies on the West Bank, see the quarterly issues of the *Journal of Palestine Studies*.

in Congress, while Israel was scheduled to receive an additional $3 billion in outright grants in FY 1986.[21]

Financial dependency on the United States has unsettling implications for Israel. In recent years, an international consensus has emerged that one of the prerequisites of international security is an even-handed settlement of the Arab-Israeli problem (i.e., one that includes self-determination for the Palestinians). A reflection of this consensus was the August 1982 U.N. General Assembly resolution that called for the right of Palestinian self-determination and national independence "in Palestine." The vote in favor of a Palestinian state was 120 to 2 (only the U.S. and Israel dissenting) with 20 abstentions. If events should cause the U.S. Congress to reorder its current pro-Israeli priorities, there is an increased likelihood that the American government—until now steadfast in its support of Israel—could begin to reflect this international consensus. A logical consequence of this shift in attitude would mean not an abandonment of Israel, but a gradual increase in acceptability of the concept that withholding military and financial aid to Israel is an appropriate means of encouraging cooperation. To the extent that Israel wants greater control over its own fate, it should take major initiatives on issues such as the Palestinian problem now rather than be subject to external pressures later.[22]

---

[21] Trudy Rubin, *Christian Science Monitor*, Dec. 8, 1981; Thomas Stauffer, *U.S. Aid to Israel: The Vital Link* (Washington, D.C.: Middle East Institute, 1983), who puts the level of U.S. aid to Israel, once all forms of assistance are accounted for, at a much higher level than official figures; "Washington's Commitment," *New York Times*, Aug. 8, 1982; George Ball, "Recast Ties to Israel," *New York Times*, July 28, 1982; David Francis, "Total U.S. Aid to Israel—its Dimensions, Implications," *Christian Science Monitor*, Aug. 9, 1982; the *Jerusalem Post* (International Edition), Nov. 17, 1984; *Christian Science Monitor*, May 1 and 3, 1985; and *CRS Issue Brief* IB84138 (Updated 04/30/85).

[22] "Demand for a Palestine State is Renewed in a Vote at U.N.," *New York Times*, Aug. 20, 1982. Many U.S. officials have expressed sentiments along these lines, including Richard Nixon, *RN, the Memoirs of Richard Nixon* (New York: Grosset & Dunlap, 1978), pp. 1007-1008.

These developments suggest that time, in the long run, is not on Israel's side. The risks of bold and meaningful initiatives for peace are dwarfed by those that could arise from a continuation of the *status quo*. The October War of 1973 made clear that maintenance of the *status quo*—which best describes the strategy followed in the aftermath of the 1967 war—was a prescription for continual unrest. On a symbolic level, the death of Anwar Sadat made the same point about the stalled autonomy talks. Neglect of the Palestinian question is not a viable policy. That problem has contributed to every major Arab-Israeli conflict. In spite of periodic attempts to downplay its salience (i.e., after the Israeli destruction of the P.L.O. military infrastructure in Beirut in 1982, again after the Syrian ouster of the P.L.O. from Tripoli in 1983, and most recently after the Palestinian-Shia conflict in Southern Lebanon in 1985), the Palestinian problem has consistently reasserted itself as an issue whose resolution is central to any long-term peace. Sizable Palestinian populations remain in Israel, Lebanon, Jordan, Gaza, and the West Bank, and the Palestinian problem, simply put, will not go away.

Although Israel's defenses are more than adequate for the near future, projections of the Arab world's population (currently over 100 million), petroleum resources (well over 350 billion barrels of proven reserves), and military capabilities suggest that in the long run Israel (with its limited resources) can only lose by failing to tackle the Palestinian question in all of its aspects. The ultimate well-being of Israel necessitates risks that can only grow with time—particularly if an unbending attitude toward the question of Palestinian self-determination, encouraged by the United States, lulls successive hardline Israeli governments into complacency and causes them to lose the opportunity for peace.

Deliberations in the 12th Palestine National Council in Algiers in February 1983 evidenced a profound concern that time, in the short run, was not on the Palestinians' side either. Gradual Israeli annexation of the occupied territories, some felt, could be prevented only if the P.L.O. responded to the Reagan initiative and sought a "state" in confederation with Jordan. Moderates arguing for a green light for Jordan's King Hussein to participate in American-sponsored peace talks hoped that, if Hussein joined the peace negotiations, the Reagan administration would give him strong support and work to obtain a full freeze on Jewish settlements in the occupied territories. Arguing against it were those who believed that painful concessions would lead nowhere in the face of Israeli intransigence and domestic American politics, leaving the P.L.O. worse off than before. In the end, the Palestine National Council refused to accept the Reagan Plan because it denied the Palestinians self-determination. The most that President Reagan had offered the Palestinians was "something in the nature of a homeland." The P.N.C. did not, however, reject the plan outright—a conscious act designed to leave the door open for negotiations. The position of the P.N.C. constituted at best a "yellow light" for King Hussein: the P.L.O. did not approve of his negotiating on its behalf, but it did not intend to attack him if he did so.[23]

Ultimately, pressures within the Palestinian movement forced Yasir Arafat to opt for the cohesion of the P.L.O. over the promise of limited self-government. Even then, his long deliberation over the choice led to destruction of the cohesion he sought to protect. Radicals supported by Syria—which has no stake in the Reagan Plan and primarily seeks to ensure that *its* interests are not overlooked—objected to Arafat's leadership as well as to his conservatism. Fearing a sell-out of what they regarded as their birthright, the radicals under Col. Said Musa started a rebellion that for a time turned into a virtual civil war within the Palestine Liberation Organization. The dissidents' ties with Syria and Arafat's expulsion from Damascus in June 1983 appeared to discredit the rebels among the P.L.O.'s 20,000 fedayeen and led to enhanced support for Arafat among the Palestinians in Lebanon, Jordan, and especially the West Bank. But massive Syrian assistance to the rebel forces in northern Lebanon forced the expulsion of the P.L.O. chairman from Tripoli in December 1983. As a result, while the Palestinian problem remains as important as ever, Arafat's authority has eroded.

The direction of the Palestinian nationalist movement, meanwhile, was subject to extended debate at the meeting of the 13th P.N.C. in Amman in November 1984, where King Hussein called on the P.L.O. to join him in seeking a negotiated settlement based on U.N. Security

---

[23]Robin Wright, *Christian Science Monitor*, Feb. 15 and 16, 1983; Trudy Rubin, *Christian Science Monitor* , Feb. 15, 18, 23, 24, 1983; Harry Ellis, *Christian Science Monitor*, Feb. 23, 1983; and Hedrick Smith, *New York Times*, Feb. 24, 1983.

Council Resolution 242. While consensus was not forthcoming in the 384-seat organization, Arafat and Hussein subsequently signed an agreement on February 11, 1985, in which Arafat apparently committed the P.L.O. (which now governs itself by majority rather than consensus) to seeking a negotiated settlement based on U.N. and Security Council resolutions. The agreement called for an international peace conference that would include a joint delegation of Jordanians and Palestinians, and stipulated that Palestinian self-determination would be sought "within the context of the formation of the proposed confederated Arab states of Jordan and Palestine." As one thoughtful commentator has observed, this means in practice "that the right of self-determination—shorthand for an independent Palestinian state—is recognized in principle, but that the need to form an association, confederation, or other arrangement between the Palestinians and Jordan is accepted as a fact."

King Hussein subsequently proposed to the United States a four-stage process for a U.S.-P.L.O. meeting, beginning with a session between the United States and a Jordanian-Palestinian delegation (excluding P.L.O. representatives), and followed by Arafat's formal declaration of his readiness to recognize and negotiate with Israel.[24] As

---

[24]For assessments of Arafat's position, see Thomas Friedman, *International Herald Tribune* , June 4 and 5, 1983; Trudy Rubin, *Christian Science Monitor*, July 6, 1983; Eric Rouleau, "The Future of the P.L.O.," *Foreign Affairs* 62 (Fall 1983), pp. 138-156; and more recently Helena Cobban, *Christian Science Monitor*, Dec. 17, 1984, Herbert Denton, *Washington Post*, Mar. 26, 1985, and Mary Curtius, *Christian Science Monitor*, June 5, 1985. Arafat's evaluation of King Hussein's discussions with President Reagan in the summer of 1985 can be found in *Palestine Perspectives* 17 (June/July 1985), pp. 4-5. See also the address by Assistant Secretary for Near Eastern and South Asian Affairs, Richard W. Murphy, *Current Policy* No. 726, Bureau of Public Affairs, U.S. Department of State, Washington, D.C., June 27, 1985, and Robert Neumann, "Middle East: America's Next Steps," *Foreign Policy* 59 (Summer 1985), pp. 106-122, for U.S. perceptions of current realities in the negotiating process; and David Ottoway, *Washington Post*, June 6, 1985, for Hussein's proposals for negotiations.

a *quid pro quo*, the United States would publicly state its support for Palestinian *self-determination* within the context of a joint Jordanian-Palestinian confederation. These details would be discussed in the first session, which would be followed by a second session between the United States and a Jordanian-Palestinian delegation (this time including P.L.O. officials). The second session would discuss an international conference (the third stage) under which direct negotiations would take place between Arabs and Israelis (the fourth stage). While several aspects of the proposal—particularly the question of whether such meetings would lead to direct talks between the joint delegation and Israel, and the notion of an international conference—posed problems for the United States, the most immediate problem, which remained unresolved at the time this monograph was written, resulted from differences over which Palestinian delegates would be acceptable to all parties.

A number of Israeli leaders, all members of the Labor Party, have indicated a sensitivity to Palestinian needs. Former Foreign Minister Abba Eban has expressed his belief that an Arab destiny on the West Bank is inevitable and that Israel should consider how best to rescue its basic interests through steps such as modest but crucial territorial change, demilitarization, military balance, and mutual accessibility. Former Prime Minister, now Defense Minister, Yitzhak Rabin has noted that the P.L.O. cannot be eliminated by force and that the only solution to the problem of Palestinian attacks must be political. Shimon Peres, before he was elected prime minister, said that if his party came to power he would seek to open talks with Jordanians and Palestinians over the future of the West Bank, and limit the construction of Israeli settlements. As prime minister, Peres has had difficulty in addressing the latter problem. Nonetheless, while he has characterized King Hussein's negotiating proposal as a ploy designed to bring about U.S. recognition of the P.L.O. and "a program for vanquishing Israel," he has outlined a five-stage plan for peace negotiations based on direct talks between Israel and a team made up of Jordanians and Palestinians not associated with the Palestine Liberation Organization. Official responsiveness to the problem posed by the Palestinians, it should be noted, is not isolated. One 1982 poll in Israel found that over half of the population favored a return of territories in exchange for peace, and a poll released by *Haaretz* in February 1985 indicated that 51.7 per cent of Israelis questioned opposed building more

West Bank settlements (a sizable shift from October 1981 when only 29.2 per cent opposed more settlements).[25]

The attitudes of the Likud coalition, on the other hand, are considerably different from those of the Labor Party. Menachem Begin, while prime minister, articulated them best when he expressed an intention to assert sovereignty over the occupied territories. During Begin's tenure in office, Israel asserted sovereignty over Syria's Golan Heights and unilaterally annexed East Jerusalem, where some 70,000-80,000 Jews now live within the expanded Jerusalem limits. During Begin's tenure, the West Bank's Jewish settlement population also increased sevenfold from 3,500 to at least 25,000, and the number of settlements more than tripled from 32 to 110.[26]

---

[25] See the editorial in the *New York Times*, June 10, 1979; David Shipler, *New York Times*, June 13, 1980; Benvenisti, *The West Bank and Gaza Data Base Project*, pp. 62-63, notes that the Labor Party supports annexation of 40 per cent of the West Bank; Hertzberg, "Israel and the West Bank," pp. 1069-1070; *Jerusalem Post*, Sept. 3, 1982; *New York Times*, Sept. 4, 1982, and Aug. 6, 1985. Of 1,937 adults interviewed, 51.2 per cent were willing to give up parts of occupied territory in return for peace; 53 per cent opposed annexation and favored compromise; 46.8 per cent, on the other hand, were opposed to giving up even one inch of territory. See also Mary Curtius, *Christian Science Monitor*, Feb. 5 and June 17, 1985; and Edward Walsh, *Washington Post*, June 11, 1985. Gloria H. Falk, "Israeli Public Opinion: Looking Toward a Palestinian Solution," *Middle East Journal* 39 (Summer 1985), pp. 247-269, cites polls by Public Opinion Research of Israel that mark a trend against new West Bank settlements from a high of 58 per cent for and 29 per cent against in October 1981 to 36 per cent for and 52 per cent against in January 1985. In a September 1984 poll cited by Falk, five per cent favored an independent Palestinian state. Her discussion of the implications of her analysis for the peace process is valuable.

[26] Trudy Rubin, *Christian Science Monitor*, Sept. 2 and 3, 1982, and Aug. 15, 1983; Ned Temko, "The Struggle for the West Bank," *Christian Science Monitor*, Jan. 4, 1982. The third Drobles Plan calls for the establishment by 1987 of 57 new settlements, 20 of which have already been approved, *Christian Science Monitor*, Aug. 17, 1983. Arthur Hertzberg has argued that by 1986 Israeli efforts, money, and settlers on the West

Meron Benvenisti asserts that the effective annexation of the West Bank has very nearly been completed. Clearly, while a consensus concerning what to do about the West Bank has yet to emerge, *de facto* annexation continues. Ze'ev Ben Yosef, spokesman for the settlement office of the World Zionist Organization, said in August 1983 that the Jewish population of the West Bank would reach 70,000 by October, when 7,000 new family apartments were taken over by their owners. The Jewish Agency's projection of 100,000 settlers on the West Bank by 1985, while overstated (in March 1985 Benvenisti's best estimate of Israeli settlers currently on the West Bank was 42,600), is within reach by 1990 if Israel's housing industry maximizes its capabilities (3,000 cheap, subsidized flats a year, housing 12,000-15,000 people). If realized, such developments will make it increasingly difficult for any Israeli government to return occupied territory to Arab control and virtually impossible to affect a political solution to the intractable Palestinian problem. As a consequence, many believe that those who desire a peaceful resolution of these issues should press Israel to terminate any new settlement activities and support creation of a Palestinian state—or, at the very least, some viable form of Palestinian self-government—in the West Bank and Gaza before it is too late.[27]

Bank will make a Palestinian state, or even an autonomous regime, impossible. "Israel and the West Bank," p. 1070. Meron Benvenisti believes that this may already be true—in part because the Likud has formed a domestic lobby made up of settlers in the bedroom suburbs and those who have an economic interest in the West Bank. This "floating vote" of 100,000, according to Likud estimates, will be an effective barrier to a political alternative espousing territorial compromise. Meron Benvenisti, "The Turning Point in Israel."

[27]"First Step to a Solution," *New Outlook*, May 1981; David Shipler, *New York Times*, Sept. 12, 1982; Trudy Rubin, *Christian Science Monitor*, Nov. 5, 10, 1982, and Aug. 17, 1983; Benvenisti, *The West Bank and Gaza Data Base Project* , p. 55; Hertzberg, "Israel and the West Bank," p. 1070; *Christian Science Monitor*, Mar. 29, 1985. For an articulate examination of a Palestinian state as being Israel's best strategic choice among relatively less appealing alternatives, see Mark Heller, *A Palestinian State: The Implications for Israel* (Cambridge, Mass.: Harvard University Press, 1983).

Arguments Opposing Palestinian Self-Determination

Creation of a Palestinian *state* in the West Bank and Gaza poses serious ideological and security problems for Isræl. Isrælis are divided over alternative solutions to the Palestinian question, but they are with few exceptions (approximately five per cent of the population) united in opposing an independent, fully-sovereign Palestinian state. As a result, many Isrælis assert that American espousal of such a policy would eliminate the credibility of the United States in Isræl, undermine its influence with Isræl in the peace process, and thereby jeopardize its interests in the region as a whole. Their reasoning illuminates the Reagan administration's advocacy of a Palestinian entity in association with Jordan. Officials in Washington did not in principle oppose the concept of self-determination; for them it was a question of what was acceptable within the context of U.S.-Isræli relations.

The Begin government, which saw such a Palestinian entity as a *potential* state and therefore rejected the Reagan Plan, believed that the conflict between Isræl's search for security and the Palestinian quest for self-determination *was* a zero-sum game. For Begin and his followers, Palestinian self-determination (which has become a codeword for an independent Palestinian state) directly challenged the government's claim to sovereignty over Eretz Isræl (the biblical land of Isræl) and threatened its very existence.[28]

Isræl's rejection of a Palestinian state and insistence on sovereignty over the occupied territories derives in part from an understandable concern for security of the Jewish state. Two thousand years of persecution and the unspeakable trauma of the holocaust, together, have instilled in the survivors what Amos Elon has called an existential sense of self-assertion in adversity. Zionist settlers who established

---

[28] Vance, *Hard Choices*, pp. 183-184.

Israel, Elon observes, were imbued with the relentless drive of drowning men who[29]

> force their way on to a life raft large enough to hold both them and those who are already in it. If they were deaf to the legal protestations of the latter, it was not only because they considered the raft a birthright but because they were swept away in a storm so ferocious that conventional legality inevitably appeared in their eyes as a tragedy and mockery of higher justice.

Former Prime Minister Begin, his successors in the government of Yitzhak Shamir, and the Likud faction in the unity government of Shimon Peres all share the beliefs and determination of those settlers described by Elon. Begin believes that Eretz Israel, including Judea and Samaria (the Biblical names he uses to refer to the West Bank), is a birthright promised in the Bible. Refusing to characterize as "occupied" what he insists is "liberated" territory ("You cannot annex your own land. This is the land of our forefathers. You annex foreign land."), Begin vowed never to divide again or hand over any part of Judea, Samaria, and East Jerusalem to foreign rule or sovereignty. Former Defense Minister Moshe Arens has declared that Israel will eventually annex the West Bank; and Yitzhak Shamir, when he was sworn in on October 10, 1983 as Israel's seventh prime minister, pledged to follow Begin's policies although he said he had no intention of annexing the West Bank. On the day he was sworn in, Shamir, referring to Israeli

---

[29] Elon, *The Israelis*, pp. 240, 259. Arthur Hertzberg, in explaining the popularity of Begin's West Bank policy among those who do not share his ideological motivations, notes that it speaks for one of the deepest emotions of world Jewry: "anger at the results of Jewish powerlessness in the age of Hitler." Hertzberg, "Israel and the West Bank," p. 1066. See also Christopher Sykes, *Crossroads to Israel*, 1917-1948 (Bloomington: Indiana University Press, 1965), pp. 269, 277, for insight into the need for redemption, the role played by the opportunity for regaining self-respect and dignity after the demoralizing cruelty perpetrated upon survivors of the "Final Solution," and the satisfaction of a religious impulse in the modern religion of patriotism.

settlements on the West Bank and Gaza, told the Knesset that "this sacred work must not stop. It is the heart of our existence and life."[30]

The dedication, conviction, and sense of righteousness of Begin, Shamir, and their supporters in the Herut Party and the Likud coalition, together with Israel's *de facto* control over the territories in question, appear to preclude any compromise on the issue of sovereignty—and particularly any compromise on the question of a Palestinian state. This interpretation was corroborated, in the wake of Begin's August 1983 decision to resign, by failed negotiations over a government of national unity, and was underscored by irreconcilable differences over settlements in September 1984 when a national unity government was formed. The denial of Palestinian self-determination, implicit in the Likud coalition's refusal to accept the more moderate position of the Labor Party on the occupied territories, follows logically from the premise of Israel's claim to Eretz Israel and is rooted in a fundamental concern: recognition of Palestinian rights would constitute acknowledgement that Jewish claims to the land of Israel were questionable. For Likud

---

[30]U.S. Congress, House, *Perspectives on the Middle East Peace-Process, Dec. 1981, Hearings, Subcommittee on Europe and the Middle East, Committee on Foreign Affairs* (Washington, D.C.:GPO, 1981), pp. 50-51, 113; *International Herald Tribune*, Sept. 9, 10, 11, 1983; Trudy Rubin, *Christian Science Monitor*, Oct. 7, 1983. Irreconcilable issues that surfaced during negotiations between Labor and the Likud following Begin's resignation included Labor's desire for the principle of territorial compromise and for limitation of new settlements to areas that Israel considered essential to its security. The Likud, of course, rejected Labor's desires. Avishai observed that Jews of Sephardic origin, many of whom come from other Arab states, now constitute 60 per cent of the voting population (and half of those who actually vote), and consistently choose Likud over Labor by a three to one margin. *New York Review of Books*, Aug. 13, 1981. For insight into what contemporary Israelis think of themselves and where they are headed, see Amos Oz, *In the Land of Israel* (New York: Harcourt Brace Jovanovich, 1983).

supporters, to divide the raft described above in Elon's metaphor, even now, would be to sink it.[31]

Numerous supporters of Israel have attempted to rationalize this existential concern through a kind of moral calculus. Barbara Tuchman has argued that Palestinian refugees should be the responsibility of the twenty-one Arab states whose population is 40 times that of Israel and whose territory is 600 times the size of Israel. She and others also suggest that Arab states should be responsible for accommodating the 725,000 refugees (a U.N. estimate) from the 1948 war, their progeny, and the refugees from the 1967 war. They see this solution to the problem of Palestinian refugees as only fair in view of the fact that Israel had to accommodate approximately 500,000 Jews displaced by Arab states in the years following the creation of Israel. More recently, some have argued that, with the return of the Sinai to Egypt, Israel gave up 92 per cent of the territory it captured in 1967; the West Bank is an insignificant part of the whole and need not be given up. These and other arguments generally proceed from the assumption that Palestinians have no distinct national identity (i.e., they are Arabs), that distinctly Palestinian claims to the land are not legitimate, or that Palestinian claims are less legitimate than those of Israel.[32]

The implications of recognizing Palestinian claims have created problems for Israeli governments. If certain beliefs are crucial to national ideology, and national ideology is regarded as central to national survival, then challenges to the legitimacy of such fundamental beliefs directly threaten the nation's capacity to sustain itself. This line of reasoning helps explain why Israeli governments—led by both Labor and Likud—have consistently denied the legitimacy of Palestinian rights and a distinctly Palestinian national identity. It explains, for

---

[31]Edward Walsh, *International Herald Tribune*, Oct. 1-2, 1983; and Trudy Rubin, *Christian Science Monitor*, Oct. 7, 1983; and *Jerusalem Post* (International Edition), Sept. 2-8, Sept. 9-15, Oct. 6, 1984.

[32]Barbara Tuchman, "A Task for the Arabs," *New York Times*, July 25, 1982; U.S. Congress, House, *Perspectives on the Middle East Peace Process*, pp. 113-114.

example, why Prime Minister Golda Meir back in 1972 prevented the inhabitants of two Arab villages in Israel from returning to their land. The issue concerned pro-Israeli Christians from Bir'im and Iqrit who had been uprooted by the Israelis, whose homes had been destroyed, and whose land had been handed over to Jewish immigrants from Iran. Their plight became a *cause célèbre* among Israeli liberals. Among the reasons the prime minister gave for preventing their return was concern that it might intensify doubts about the righteousness of the Zionist cause. She feared that these doubts might contribute to an erosion of Zionist ideology and prove to be a danger—perhaps Israel's greatest—against which "not even Phantom fighter planes can help."[33]

The threat posed by any compromise on the issue of historical rights and sovereignty is central to the concerns of the Likud coalition, and it helps explain the assertions of Yitzhak Shamir, Moshe Arens, and former Defense Minister Ariel Sharon that "Jordan is Palestine."[34]

---

[33]Joseph Ryan, "Refugees Within Israel: The Case of the Villagers of Kafr Bir'im and Iqrit," *Journal of Palestine Studies* 2 (Summer 1973), pp. 55-81.

[34]Trudy Rubin and Daniel Southerland, *Christian Science Monitor*, Sept. 2, 1982; George Will's columns in the *Washington Post*, Sept. 2, 5, 9, 1982; U.S. Congress, House, *Perspectives on the Middle East Peace Process*, p. 51. After President Reagan called for a "homeland" for the Palestinians on the West Bank, Arens' response was emphatic: "Israel's position is that a Palestinian homeland and state exists—Jordan." Cited in *Link* 16 (May/June 1983), p. 2. For an elaboration of the argument that Jordan is an integral part (77 per cent) of what was known as Palestine, that exclusive application of the term "Palestine" to the inhabitants of the West Bank is a semantic exercise to undermine the legitimacy of Israel, and that Trans-Jordan, or eastern Palestine, is the Palestinian homeland, see Yitzhak Shamir, "Israel's Role in a Changing World," *Foreign Affairs* 60 (Spring 1982), pp. 789-801. Some of these matters are clarified by Bernard Lewis, "The Palestinians and the PLO: A Historical Approach," *Commentary* 59 (Jan. 1975), pp. 32-46, and by L. Dean Brown, *The Land of Palestine: West Bank Not East Bank* (Washington, D.C.: Middle East Institute, 1982), which underscores the speciousness of the "Jordan is Palestine" campaign.

Following World War I, what is now Jordan was part of the land designated as Palestine and mandated to the British by the League of Nations. It was later separated from the Palestine mandate by the British, who restricted application of the Balfour Declaration to the region west of the Jordan River. While the British had no intention then of creating a predominantly Jewish state in all of this smaller area, many Israelis now apparently do. Because of the influx of Palestinian refugees from various Arab-Israeli wars, a majority of Jordan's population (approximately 65 per cent) is now Palestinian. Relating this demographic development to the tenuous designation of Jordan as Palestine, some Israelis, including Sharon, welcome a Palestinian takeover of Amman. The resulting partition of "Palestine," for this group, would absolve Israel of having to make further territorial concessions and would be consistent with Israeli claims to sovereignty over the West Bank and Gaza.[35]

Many Israelis, particularly supporters of the Labor Party who do not necessarily reject a Palestinian state on ideological grounds, still reject this course for reasons of security. The worst Israeli fear is that a radical Palestinian state, with Soviet and Arab support, would attempt to realize the goals articulated in the 1968 Palestine National Covenant

---

[35] Arthur Hertzberg, *New York Review of Books* , Oct. 21, 1982. As Hertzberg has noted elsewhere, grandiose political thinking along the lines of Sharon's is dangerously naive. Political disintegration of neighboring states is likely to give Israel neighbors that are even less favorably disposed toward Israel than the ones they now have; radicalization of the Arab world would not be in Israel's best interests. "Israel and the West Bank," pp. 1072, 1074. For discussion of the Balfour Declaration, see Leonard Stein, *The Balfour Declaration* (New York: Simon & Schuster, 1961); Ronald Sanders, *The High Walls of Jerusalem: A History of the Balfour Declaration and the Birth of the British Mandate for Palestine* (New York: Holt, Rinehart & Winston, 1983), and the thoughtful review in the *New York Review of Books*, Mar. 15, 1984, which points out its one glaring deficiency. The Balfour Declaration, an important source of legitimacy for Israel, was quoted in full in the British Mandate for Palestine, which was sanctioned by the League of Nations.

and adopted by the Palestine National Council. Palestinian endorsement of armed struggle to liberate and exercise sovereignty over "Palestine" (i.e., Israel *and* the occupied territories) heightens Israeli anxieties and reinforces the Israeli belief that no compromise is possible.[36]

Israeli apprehensions about military security are well-founded. Since World War II, over 10,000 Israelis have been killed in battle against Arab foes.[37] Terrorism has also taken its toll. According to

---

[36]Excerpts from the Covenant along with the Palestine National Council's Ten Point Program are reprinted in Wolf Blitzer, ed., *Myths and Facts, 1976* (Washington, D.C.: Near East Report, 1976), pp. 72-79.

[37]According to Trevor Dupuy, the number of Arabs and Israelis killed in action in the various Arab-Israeli Wars is:

	ISRAELIS	ARABS
1948	6,000	15,000
1956	189	1,650
1967	983	4,296
1967-1970	627	5,000
1973	2,838	8,528
TOTAL	10,637	34,474

Elusive Victory: The Arab-Israeli Wars, 1947-74 (New York: Harper & Row, 1978), pp. 124, 212, 333, 369, 609. By contrast, the wars in neighboring states have been far more costly: most estimates put the number of lives lost in the Jordan civil war at 10,000. According to David Gordon, *Lebanon: The Fragmented Nation* (London: Croom Helm, 1980), p. 235, the Lebanese civil war of 1975-1976 cost 50-60,000 human lives. Walid Khalidi, on the other hand, sees such a number as wide of the mark and accepts an estimate of 30,000. See *Conflict and Violence in Lebanon: Confrontation in the Middle East* (Cambridge, Mass.: Center for International Affairs, Harvard University, 1979), pp. 104, 174. One reasonably reliable estimate of the lives lost during the 1982 Palestinian-Israeli War in Lebanon puts the number of Arab lives lost at 17,825 (*New York Times*, Sept. 2, 1982). The number of victims (as many as half of whom were Lebanese Shiites) in the massacres at Sabra and Shatila is subject to dispute, ranging from 460 to 1,000. See David Ottoway, *International Herald Tribune*, Sept. 19, 1983. As for Israeli deaths, the Israelis in

statistics compiled by the Israeli Defense Forces, in the years from 1967 to 1980 there were a total of 3,174 terrorist attacks in the occupied territories and 1,306 in Israel. In the course of these attacks, 230 Israelis were killed and 3,303 injured. For many Israelis, the lesson of these statistics is clear: Israel cannot afford the luxury of trusting a sovereign Palestinian state. Creation of such a state would leave Israel with a narrow strip of land connecting its northern and southern territories; it would expose 80 per cent of Israel's population to long-range guns and rockets in the West Bank.

From an Israeli perspective, territory and security are closely related. The West Bank is essential as a buffer; control over it provides reasonable assurance that it will not serve as a springboard for a large-scale attack on Israel; access to it allows Israel to place early warning and control systems and to deploy military forces along the Jordan Valley and in the central mountain range. Palestinian sovereignty over the West Bank would decrease Israel's capacity to safeguard its security through these mechanisms of control. Road networks, constructed with Israel's defense in mind, and groundwater aquifers, whose mismanagement would cause irreversible salination of the aquifers in Israel's plains, would be subject to Palestinian control. Palestinian jurisdiction over Israeli actions on the West Bank, moreover, would cause hopeless complications, making an effective Israeli defense extremely difficult. Relinquishing exclusive Israeli control over Jerusalem, the focal point of Jewry throughout history, would pose severe security risks. Israelis also remember only too well that between 1948 and 1967 Jordan denied Israeli/Jewish access to the holy places in East Jerusalem under Jordanian occupation. As a result, if Palestinian sovereignty were not strictly qualified to the point where it became almost meaningless,

---

early September 1982 reported 340 killed and 2,200 wounded in action (Ed Walsh, *Washington Post*, Sept. 6, 1982). On the eve of Israeli withdrawal in June 1985, Israeli losses were reported as 654 dead and 3,195 wounded (Marty Curtius, *Christian Science Monitor*, June 4, 1985). For the impact of terrorism, see Daniel Elazar, ed., *Judea, Samaria, and Gaza: Views on the Present and the Future* (Washington, D.C.: American Enterprise Institute, 1982), p. 188. For another estimate see Michael Jansen, *The Battle of Beirut: Why Israel Invaded Lebanon* (Boston: South End Press, 1982), p. 130.

Isræl would be forced to return to a pre-1967 strategy of pre-emptive attacks when it felt sufficiently threatened.[38]

The difficulties associated with a strategy of pre-emption are suggested by the fact that Isræl, in spite of possessing the plan for Operation Badr, was subject to strategic surprise during the 1973 War. Richard Betts attributes Isræl's surprise to several factors: excessive reliance on the military balance of forces, an underestimation of ideological and psychological factors, the consequences of "alert fatigue," and a reliance on strategic preconceptions that degraded the perception of tactical indicators. Clearly, without a territorial buffer (let alone a canal, to protect its eastern flank), Isræl would constantly face the difficult task of interpreting risks. As the October war illustrated, this is no easy matter. Isræl would also constantly have to assess the question of how much evidence warranted the costs involved in pre-emptive military action. These costs would be enormous—both for Isræl and for regional stability.[39]

Terrorism presents Isræl with an additional problem. Major General Rephæl Vardi, a former head of the military government in the occupied territories and later comptroller of the Isræli Defense Establishment, believes that an effective strategy against terrorism necessitates freedom of action on the West Bank. Bitter experiences with terrorists have taught Isræl that orderly life requires internal security. Internal security, in turn, requires a strategy of reprisals that places responsibility for terror on the states from which it originates. If one accepts Vardi's analysis, Isræli security requirements are incompatible with the concept of Palestinian sovereignty.[40]

------

[38] For discussion of Isræli concern for water resources, see J. Schwartz, "Water Resources in Judea, Samaria, and the Gaza Strip," in Elazar, *Judea, Samaria, and Gaza*, pp. 81-100; Benvenisti, *The West Bank and Gaza*, pp. 19-23; John Cooley, "The War over Water," *Foreign Policy* 54 (Spring 1984), pp. 3-26; and Leslie C. Schmida, "Isræl's Drive for Water," *Link* 17 (Nov. 1984).

[39] Richard Betts, *Strategic Surprise* (Washington, D.C.: Brookings Institution, 1982), pp. 68-80, 104.

[40] Rephæl Vardi, "The Administered Territories and the Internal Security of Isræl," in Elazar, *Judea, and Samaria, and Gaza*, pp. 171-190. The relative severity of Isræli reprisals is indicated by

For some Isrælis, the problems associated with implementing an agreement on a Palestinian state, even if the sovereignty issue were capable of being resolved, are virtually insurmountable. What guarantees would Isræl have? Who would ensure those guarantees? United Nations actions in recent years have failed to give Isræl any confidence in that body. United States guarantees are also suspect. Isrælis were not impressed by previous American commitments concerning the Straits of Tiran, nor were they pleased with the United States failure to monitor and then address Egyptian violations of the cease-fire between Isræl and Egypt in 1970.

When American Marines participated in the Lebanon peace-keeping force in the first months of 1983, Isræli officials complained that American troops were acting as a buffer behind which P.L.O. terrorists were withdrawing after ambushing Isræli troops. The withdrawal of American troops from Lebanon in early 1984 further undermined confidence in the will of the United States to sustain a commitment in the Middle East. If Europeans occasionally doubt U.S. commitments to NATO, how could Isræl doubt American commitments any less?

The refugee problem also poses practical difficulties for many Isrælis. Isræl, they believe, should exercise at least some control over Palestinian immigration. If a Palestinian state were established, who could return? How many? Who would monitor the process? If all Palestinians chose to come back to a new state, its absorptive capacity would be overtaxed and the immigrants could stimulate irredentism—either toward Isræl or toward Jordan (approximately 65 per cent of whose population, as we have noted, is Palestinian). The latter course could result in a radical Palestinian-Jordanian state. In any case, instability would be chronic. Arabs in Isræl would demand incorporation in a Palestinian state, while the status of Isræli settlers on the West Bank would present constant problems. The trauma of removing 2,000 settlers from Yamit in the Sinai in April 1982 and the costs, both emotional and monetary, that were involved suggest the kinds of

---

one estimate that between the October 1973 war and the 1978 invasion of Lebanon, the number of Isrælis killed by Palestinians was 143, while the number of Palestinians and Lebanese killed by Isræli reprisals was 2,000 (*Time*, Mar. 27, 1978).

problems that would be posed by this issue which, like most issues in Israel, has security implications. As Israeli Attorney General Aharon Barak told President Carter at Camp David, settlers can serve as justification for the movement of Israeli forces into a region. This is one reason why Israel does not intend to remove its settlers from the West Bank. Yamit, former Defense Minister Ariel Sharon has stated, is the "Red Line" of Israeli concessions.[41]

If all these issues could be resolved, a Palestinian state would still face serious problems. What would ensure its moderation? The experience of the Arab Deterrent Force (A.D.F.) and the United Nations Interim Force (U.N.I.F.I.L.) in Lebanon is not promising. Many Israelis fear that the political and social gaps inherent in Palestinian society would quickly manifest themselves and serve as a source of instability. Would such an entity be economically viable? A small, poor state would be vulnerable to external manipulation by a host of countries, such as Syria, that have supported dissident factions within the P.L.O. and that bear Israel ill-will. How could one control external aid? Feuds between rivals such as Syria and Iraq, and struggles between moderate and radical power alignments would play themselves out in a Palestinian state. Restrictions on military forces and weapons have never worked and would be resented. Verification would be a constant problem and would only stimulate nationalist fervor.

Israelis also worry that rejectionist groups such as the National Palestinian Salvation Front or subsets of this coalition of guerrilla factions, such as George Habash's Popular Front for the Liberation of Palestine (P.F.L.P.), would see a small state as only the first step in realizing long-term Palestinian goals, and play on unfulfilled nationalist yearnings for a democratic, secular state in all of Palestine. They doubt that the state could control their attacks on Israel from bases in the state. Yasir Arafat was unable to curb the P.L.O., and King Hussein could not control the Palestinians in Jordan in 1970-71.[42]

---

[41]Jimmy Carter, *Keeping Faith: Memoirs of a President* (New York: Bantam Books, 1982), p. 382; John Yemma, *Christian Science Monitor*, Apr. 26, 1982.

[42]Cooley, *Green March, Black September*, pp. 108 ff

Arafat's recent difficulties in Lebanon with the Abu-Musa-led rebellion within the ranks of the P.L.O. are hardly reassuring, particularly since Syria's President Hafez al-Assad has made it clear that there can be no solution to the Palestinian problem without addressing Syrian interests. Syrian support for dissident activities within a Palestinian state and promotion of attacks against Isræl from that state would force the Isrælis to retaliate. The consequences of Isræli retaliatory policies would only add fuel to the fire. Eventually, many Isrælis believe, whatever Palestinian government there was would fall or be overthrown, and the Palestinians subsequently would renege on their agreements. Chaos would reign.

The issue of sovereignty, for many different reasons, is at the heart of Isræli objections to a Palestinian state. As a review of recent attempts by the United States to mediate the problem will show, matters relating to the issue of sovereignty continue to be a major constraint in devising a constructive solution to the Palestinian question. Before turning to the role of the U.S. as mediator, however, it may be instructive to examine in some detail the process by which the United States first became involved in the Palestinian question in order to appreciate the implications of that involvement and the consequent responsibilities of the United States to both sides in the conflict.

II

THE ORIGINS AND IMPLICATIONS OF U.S INVOLVEMENT IN THE PALESTINIAN PROBLEM

Britain's so-called "equality of obligation" to Arabs and Jews, enshrined in the Balfour Declaration in 1917 and incorporated after World War I in the British Mandate for Palestine, committed the British to "view with favour the establishment in Palestine of a national home for the Jewish people...it being clearly understood that nothing shall be done which may prejudice the civil and religious rights of the existing non-Jewish [i.e., Arab] communities in Palestine...."[43] When the British government in 1947 decided to give up its mandate and depart from Palestine, Foreign Minister Ernest Bevin based his decision on the conclusion that the British could not reconcile these two obligations without American support and on the belief that the United States could not be relied upon to support a settlement that failed to satisfy the proponents of Zionism.[44]

---

[43]For the Palestinian case, see fn. 4.

[44]For background on British policy during the Mandate, see Christopher Sykes, *Crossroads to Isræl, 1917-1948* (Bloomington, Ind.:University of Indiana Press, 1965), and Michæl Cohen, *Palestine and the Great Powers, 1945-1948* (Princeton, N.J.: Princeton University Press, 1982). See also Alan Bullock, *Ernest Bevin: Foreign Secretary, 1945-1951* (New York: Norton, 1983), esp. pp. 44, 646, and 841. For U.S. commitment, see *Foreign Relations of the United States: Diplomatic Papers*, 1948, Vol. V (Washington, D.C.: GPO, 1975, 1976), pp. 690-691. Hereafter, all references to this series will be cited in the following format: *FR*, year, volume number in Roman numerals, pages.

Britain's equality of obligation was shared to some extent by the United States. President Woodrow Wilson secretly approved the Balfour declaration before it was officially sent, and a joint resolution of Congress approved it in 1922. President Roosevelt, moreover, subsequently undertook two additional and equally irreconcilable commitments. On the one hand he endorsed the idea of a Jewish state, and on the other he promised King Abd Al-Aziz Ibn Saud that he would neither do anything to help the Jews against the Arabs nor take any action in his capacity as president which might prove hostile to the Arab people. When President Truman took office and inherited the contradictory commitments of his predecessors, he might well have echoed Prime Minister Ramsay MacDonald's observation to David Lloyd George in a debate over Palestine in 1930 when the latter accused him of breaking the word of England: "It was not a word we inherited. We inherited words, and they are not always consistent."[45]

Compounding the problems posed by this legacy of equivocation were several additional factors that contributed to the inconsistencies in U.S. policies toward Palestine: President Truman's empathy for survivors of the Holocaust, White House responsiveness to the interests and concerns of the American Jewish community, and the State Department's sensitivity to the broad regional context within which U.S. policy toward Palestine would be implemented. Together these factors presented government officials with a fundamental problem that has been with them ever since: humanitarian concerns, domestic political priorities, and wide-ranging interests in the emerging third world, though not always compatible with each other, had to be reconciled in the context of the "national interest."

Regional specialists in the Department of State, whose professional training and responsibilities made them especially sensitive to the concerns of the Arabs, believed that the national interest required good relations with the Arab world. As a result, they worried that U.S. support for Zionist goals would alienate the Arabs, make them more

---

[45]Ronald Sanders, *The High Walls of Jerusalem*, p. 598; Cordell Hull, *Memoirs of Cordell Hull* II (New York: Macmillan, 1948), p. 1536; Evan Wilson, *Decision on Palestine: How the U.S. Came to Recognize Israel* (Stanford, Calif.: Hoover Institution, 1979), pp. 45, 51, 180-81; Sykes, *Crossroad to Israel*, pp. 118.

receptive to the Soviets, and undermine America's evolving efforts to contain Soviet influence along the Middle East's "Northern Tier" of states. "There is no use in strengthening the arch [in Greece, Turkey, and Iran]," Director of the Division of Near Eastern Affairs Gordon Merriam wrote in October 1946, "if we are going to kick out the pillars." Loy Henderson, Director of the Office of Near Eastern and African Affairs (N.E.A.), agreed. A hostile attitude on the part of the Arabs, he wrote Under Secretary of State Robert Lovett in August 1947, "would threaten from the rear the position we are desperately trying to hold in Greece, Turkey, and Iran." A later report by the Policy Planning Staff assessing the U.S. position on Palestine in light of the partition proposal (discussed below) by the United Nations Special Committee on Palestine (U.N.S.C.O.P.), elaborated upon this consistent concern: the proposal, if implemented, would afford the Soviets an opportunity to introduce forces into Palestine, outflank U.S. positions along the Middle East's Northern Tier, threaten the stability of the entire Eastern Mediterranean, and undermine the whole structure of security that had been set up in the Near East at the time of the Truman Doctrine. [46]

Officials in N.E.A. were sensitive to the plight of displaced persons (D.P.s) but they did not see Palestine as the exclusive solution to the problems confronted by European Jewry. In their view, the Jewish D.P. problem, if it were to be solved, required a comprehensive worldwide scheme as well as an acceptable solution to the Palestine problem as a whole. The Jewish D.P. problem was not within N.E.A.'s bureaucratic domain and explains in part why officials in Henderson's office were only incidentally concerned with aiding

---

[46]Oct. 15, 1946 memo from Gordon Merriam to Loy Henderson, a xeroxed copy of which is in the author's possession; Wilson, *Decision on Palestine*, pp. 99-100; *FR*, 1947, V: 800; and *FR*, 1948, V, 545-555; and Kenneth Ray Bain, *The March to Zion: United States Policy and the Founding of Israel* (College Station, Tex.: Texas A&M University Press, 1979), p. 62. For the Turkish consul in Jerusalem's echo of this perception see *FR*, 1948, V: 1030. For discussion of the background of the Truman Doctrine, see Bruce Kuniholm, *The Origins of the Cold War in the Near East:Great Power Conflict and Diplomacy in Iran, Turkey, and Greece* (Princeton, N.J.:Princeton University Press, 1980).

Holocaust survivors. N.E.A. judged the survivors' goal of establishing a Jewish state to be antithetical to U.S. interests. Finding an acceptable solution to the Palestine problem, on the other hand, was one of their primary concerns, and like their British counterparts they believed it could be achieved only on the basis of consent by *both* Arabs and Jews. Political questions, in short, had to be settled first. This explains N.E.A.'s initial attachment to the notion of a binational state. Without the consent of both parties, Merriam and Henderson believed, the principle of self-determination, so deeply imbedded in U.S. foreign policy, would be violated and the U.N. Charter itself contravened.[47]

In November 1947 the United Nations General Assembly recommended adoption of the U.N.S.C.O.P. majority plan for the partition of Palestine. Arab rejection of this recommendation, however, led officials in N.E.A. to conclude that partition was incapable of being implemented except by force. Since President Truman did not intend to deploy forces in Palestine, and many in the State Department and the Pentagon advised against it, officials further concluded that partition was unworkable; it would result, they believed, in bloodshed, serious unrest, and instability, which the Soviet Union could readily exploit. Partition not only would require a long-term U.S. commitment but would damage overall U.S. security interests, which included Arab friendship, strategic lodgements in the Middle East, and access to Arabian oil.[48]

Loy Henderson, who like the British had come to believe that there was no solution to which both Jews and Arabs would acquiesce, had

---

[47]Oct. 15, 1946 memo from Merriam to Henderson; Wilson, *Decision on Palestine*, pp. 37, 155; Bain, *The March of Zion*, pp. 65, 200. In 1948 Arnold Toynbee told the Council on Foreign Relations that the partition of Palestine was "the *reductio ad absurdum* of territorial nationality." Peter Grose, *Israel in the Mind of America* (New York: Knopf, 1983), pp. 263, 345. It is worth noting that only two Asian countries (India and Iran) were on the United Nations Special Committee on Palestine (U.N.S.C.O.P.) and that they opposed the majority plan.

[48]*FR*, 1948, V: 545-562, 573-581, 600-603, 619-625. On the question of force deployment, see *FR*, 1945, VIII: 724-5, 742-3; *FR*, 1946, VII: 644-5; *FR*, 1948, V: 797-800; Dean Acheson, *Present at the Creation: My Years in the State*

reluctantly gone along with partition. He continued to think, however, that a workable solution could evolve only after long and protracted discussion during which moderates could find common ground. This process, he believed, would be impeded by the U.S. taking sides (i.e., support for partition), but could be encouraged under trusteeship. When the situation in Palestine began to deteriorate in late 1947, Henderson's office looked once again at the possibility of a trusteeship. "[A]lthough there are many doubts about trusteeship," Merriam wrote Henderson in the Spring of 1948, "no one has anything better to offer...." A compromise solution, however, if it ever had a chance, by this time had no hope. On the day after the United States proposed in the United Nations that partition be delayed, David Ben-Gurion, Chairman of the Jewish Agency Executive, observed that the establishment of a Jewish state did not depend on the U.N. partition resolution but on the Jews' ability to emerge victorious: "It is we," he said, "who will decide the fate of Palestine." U.S. policy, in effect, had become irrelevant to events in Palestine.[49]

The Department of State's management of the Palestine question has been the subject of considerable criticism, some of which is merited. In the judgment of one historian, State and Pentagon officials exaggerated the *immediate* danger to U.S. oil interests and overestimated Soviet capacity to meddle in the region. While this may be true, subsequent events have demonstrated that the *long-term* danger to Western oil interests was not exaggerated. Soviet options in the region, moreover, if overestimated at the time, were significantly

---

Department (New York: Norton, 1969), p. 179; Harry S. Truman, *Years of Trial and Hope* (Garden City, N.Y.: Doubleday, 1956), pp. 149, 162; Cohen, *Palestine and the Great Powers, 1945-1948*, p. 394; Robert J. Donovan, *Conflict and Crisis: The Presidency of Harry S Truman, 1945-1948* (New York: Norton, 1977), p. 313.

[49]*FR*, 1947, V: 1153-58, 1264-6, 1313-14; Aaron Miller, *Search for Security: Saudi Arabian Oil and American Foreign Policy, 1939-1949* (Chapel Hill, N.C.: University of North Carolina Press, 1980), p. 194; Wilson, *Decision on Palestine*, pp. 155-6; Grose, *Isræl in the Mind of America*, p. 275; Cohen *Palestine and the Great Powers, 1945-1948*, p. 335.

expanded under Stalin's successors—in part because of the legacy of U.S. policy toward the Palestine problem.[50]

More cogent, perhaps, is the criticism that American diplomats, who were endlessly impressed by demonstrations and editorials in Arab capitals, derided similar expressions in their own country as "playing politics." The result was a failure to develop an approach that accounted for popular sentiments in its recognition of realistic alternatives. Evan Wilson, who served on the Palestine desk in the 1940's, acknowledges that N.E.A. thinking did not sufficiently account for the domestic political imperatives that were relevant to the Palestine question. "Nor did it take sufficiently into account," Wilson adds, "...the driving force of nationalism among both Arabs and Jews." This failure—and in particular the failure either to comprehend the significance of the Holocaust for world Jewry or to understand its implications for Zionism—led State Department officials to believe that a compromise solution in Palestine was feasible when it may have been impossible. In Wilson's retrospective judgment a solution along the lines of a binational state was simply not an option after World War II. A failure to understand the imperatives of Zionism also led department officials to be overly optimistic about the ability of the United Nations to resolve disputes. In Wilson's view, a Jewish state was bound to come.[51]

---

[50]Ibn Saud, in a letter to Truman, had warned the United States in October 1947 that support for partition would result in a death blow to American interests in Arab countries, and the Arab League apparently considered the possibility of cancelling British and American concessions in the Arab world. In spite of these alarms, however, the King's immediate economic interests were bound up with the United States. Miller, *Search for Security*, pp. XVII, 147, 169-70, 187-88, 190, 209-10, 282.

[51]Grose, *Israel in the Mind of America*, p. 215; Bain, *The March of Zion*, p. 91; Donovan, *Conflict and Crisis*, p. 378; Wilson, *Decision on Palestine*, pp. 37, 151, 155-57. Bain, *The March of Zion*, pp. 199, 213, argues that the U.N. offered prospects for a collective solution to the Jewish refugee problem that could have minimized future conflict and made possible a just settlement. This judgment ignores, however, the strength of Jewish nationalism. Any compromise solution in Palestine, moreover, would have been difficult because it would have been opposed by both Arabs and Jews.

Finally, the State Department was seriously misinformed about the military situation in Palestine. General George Marshall, for example, saw grave risks and warned the Jewish Agency's Moshe Shertok against relying on the advice of his military. "Believe me, I am talking about things which I know," Marshall told him. "You are sitting there in the coastal plains of Palestine while the Arabs hold the mountain ridges.... [T]he Arabs have regular armies. They are well trained and they have heavy arms. How can you hope to hold out?" In March 1951, Marshall noted in a cabinet meeting that twice in his career he had been seriously misinformed on the military potentialities of foreign powers. The first instance was the power of the French army in 1940; the second was the grave overestimate of Arab military strength in the recent conflict with Isræl. The latter, he observed, constituted a gross failure of military intelligence. In 1947-1948, needless to say, misinformation clearly complicated the judgment of N.E.A. officials who among other objectives were also seeking to avert what they felt was an impending bloodbath.[52]

President Truman during these years was never convinced by the State Department's arguments on the Palestine question. His humanitarian instincts and attachment to the Bible inclined him, in spite of occasional irritability at Zionist pressures, to be sympathetic to the Jewish people's need to build a new life. Officials in the Department of State, he felt, were more concerned with the goodwill of the Arabs and the danger of antagonizing them than with the suffering of the Jews. It was his belief that he could help the victims of the Holocaust find a home in Palestine, protect his political future in the United States, *and* safeguard the interests of the United States in the Middle East.[53]

---

[52]Grose, *Isræl in the Mind of America,* p. 287; Memorandum for the President, March 15, 1951, President's Secretary's Files, Harry S. Truman Papers, Truman Library; Wilson, *Decision on Palestine,* p. 157.

[53]Truman, *Years of Trial and Hope,* pp. 135, 140, 145; Cohen, *Palestine and the Great Powers, 1945-1948,* pp. 53-54, 167; Zvi Ganin, *Truman, American Jewry, and Isræl, 1945-1948* (New York: Holmes & Meier, 1979), pp. xv, 105; Grose, *Isræl in the Mind of America,* p. 217; Miller, *Search for Security,* p. 199.

Explanations for the president's view deserve brief elaboration. To begin with, he did not fully understand either the history of the Palestine question or the dilemma inherent in the Balfour Declaration. This explains, perhaps, why he failed on occasion to comprehend the distinction between one diplomatic formula and another. Nor did he appreciate the perspective of the Arabs themselves. Unlike Roosevelt, he was not sensitive to the akwardness of asking Arabs to accept Jewish immigrants in Palestine when the U.S. was reluctant to do so. Nor was he sensitive to the fact that the admission of displaced Jews into Palestine or the creation of a Jewish state in Palestine represented actions that the Arabs had legitimate reason to regard as hostile.[54]

President Truman, because of his limited understanding of the Arab world, seems also to have been unwarrantedly optimistic about Palestine. Partition, for example, he initially regarded as opening the way for peaceful collaboration along the lines of the Tennessee Valley Authority between Arabs and Jews. In this, he was no different from many liberal Democrats such as Eleanor Roosevelt who, in opposition to Loy Henderson's warnings in 1947 about the U.N. majority plan, declared: "Come, come, Mr. Henderson. I think you're exaggerating the dangers. You are too pessimistic. A few years ago Ireland was considered to be a problem that could not be solved. Then the Irish Republic was established and the problem vanished. I'm confident that when a Jewish state is set up, the Arabs will see the light; they will quiet down; and Palestine will no longer be a problem."[55]

While the president was intent on doing what was "right" when it came to Palestine, an objective view was difficult to achieve because the environment in which President Truman operated, as Ernest Bevin

---

[54]Transcript of interview with Harry N. Howard, Truman Library; Grose, *Israel in the Mind of America,* pp. 146, 294-6; Truman, *Years of Trial and Hope,* pp. 132-3, 156, 164. *FR,* 1946, VII: 714-17.

[55]Truman, *Years of Trial and Hope,* p. 156; and transcript of interview with Loy Henderson, Truman Library; Wilson, *Decision on Palestine,* pp. 116, 214; Bain, *The March of Zion* , pp. 62, 202. Roosevelt, interestingly enough, considered himself something of an expert on the Middle East and believed he could straighten it out. For Roosevelt's views on Palestine, see Wilson, Ch. 4, and Grose, *Israel in the Mind of America,* Chs. 5 and 6.

recognized, was overwhelmingly supportive of the Zionist cause. The American Zionist Emergency Council (A.Z.E.C.) and its 400 local committees, their prominence among Jews of the world accentuated by the virtual disappearance of European Jewry, worked hard in pressing the Zionist case. The White House, in the last half of 1947, for example, received 135,000 communications regarding Palestine and during one three-month period in 1948 received over 300,000 postcards, nearly all of which came from Jewish interest groups and their supporters. As a result of A.Z.E.C.'s efforts, 33 state legislatures passed resolutions favoring a Jewish state in Palestine, while 40 governors, 54 senators, and 250 congressmen signed petitions to the president.[56]

Zionists also set about "educating" Truman's former business partner Eddie Jacobson to gain access to Truman. At the recommendation of the president's administrative assistant David Niles they focussed their attention on Special Counsel Clark Clifford and found an avenue to Clifford through his pro-tem aide Max Lowenthal. They briefed Niles and Clifford regularly, providing material that served as a basis for many memoranda to the president and even drafting some of Truman's statements. Truman, at times, appears to have been unaware of the work of his aides, whose actions in lobbying heavily for the partition of Palestine, for example, were at odds with instructions the president gave to the Department of State. The president's role in this episode, needless to say, is the subject of considerable controversy.[57]

The President's responsiveness to Zionist influence was, aside from his emotional predispositions, based on political reality. "I have to answer to hundreds of thousands who are anxious for the success of

---

[56] James McDonald's report on a conversation with the president, July 27, 1946, Clark Clifford Papers, Library; John Snetsinger, *Truman, the Jewish Vote and the Creation of Isræl* (Stanford, Calif.: Hoover Institution, 1974), pp. 5-6; Wilson, *Decision on Palestine*, p. 115; Grose, *Isræl in the Mind of America*, p. 191; and *FR*, 1948, V: 691.

[57] Grose, *Isræl in the Mind of America*, pp. 230-31, 248-54, 270-71; Cohen *Palestine and the Great Powers, 1945-1948* , pp. 46, 162-63, 292-300, 354n13; Wilson, *Decision on Palestine*, p. 98, 125-27; Ganin, *Truman, American Jewry, and Isræl*, pp. 142-46; Donovan, *Conflict and Crisis*, p. 329.

Zionism," he told a number of State Department representatives on one occasion, "I do not have hundreds of thousands of Arabs among my constituents." Historians have pointed out numerous occasions in which Zionist pressures, both direct and indirect, influenced his decisions. These include rejection of the Morrison-Grady plan, the president's Yom Kippur speech in 1946, support for the partition of Palestine in 1947, and the decision to recognize Israel in 1948.

Clark Clifford, one of his key advisors, has contested the assertion of one historian that Truman's policies were motivated by short term political expediency rather than long-range national goals, arguing that political factors played only a minor role in Truman's broad national strategy for reelection in 1948. Clifford has cited as a case in point a memo he submitted to the president in November 1947 in which he argued that decisions on the Palestine problem should be founded upon intrinsic merit. He neglected to mention, however, his observations in that memo that the Jewish vote was important in New York, that no candidate since 1876 (except for Wilson in 1916) had lost New York and won the presidency, and that its 47 electoral votes were the first prize in any election. He also failed to point out that while the president lost New York in 1948, he won Ohio, California and Illinois; in each of these states, the Jewish vote was crucial to his election.[58]

Another factor that complicated the president's determination to do what was right was the predisposition of his advisors in the White House to share widely accepted stereotypes of Arabs. "You know that President Roosevelt said to some of us privately he could do anything that needed to be done with Ibn Saud with a few million dollars," the president's assistant David Niles wrote him in May 1946, failing to note that this judgment had changed considerably after Roosevelt's

---

[58]November 19, 1947 memo from Clifford to Truman, Clark Clifford Papers, Truman Library; Cohen, *Palestine and the Great Powers, 1945-1948*, pp. 46-47, 58, 64, 65n, 113, 128-132, 164-66; Grose, *Israel in the Mind of America*, pp. 216, 288-293, 300-301; Ganin, *Truman, American Jewry, and Israel*, pp. 144-45; Donovan, *Conflict and Crisis*, p. 320; Bain, *The March to Zion*, p. 202; *FR*, 1946, VII: 682-83; Wilson, *Decision on Palestine*, pp. 123, 142-43; Truman, *Years of Trial and Hope*, p. 158; Ganin, p. 101; Snetsinger, *Truman, the Jewish Vote, and the Creation of Palestine*, pp. 120-140; Clark Clifford, speech before the American Historical Association, Dec. 22, 1976, Washington, D.C.

meeting with the king in February 1945. In that same memo Niles asserted that there would be very little opposition to the transfer of 100,000 displaced European Jews to Palestine and discounted the danger of unifying Muslims by such action on the grounds that "a good part of the Moslem world follows Gandhi and his philosophy of nonresistance." In another memo to the president, Clark Clifford noted that the United States appeared "in the ridiculous role of trembling before threats of a few nomadic desert tribes.... Why should Russia or Yugoslavia, or any other nation treat us with anything but contempt," he wrote, "in light of our shilly-shallying appeasement of the Arabs." This kind of advice from aides who had no sympathy for and knew little about the Arabs may well have influenced the president, when he was confronted by domestic pressures and political constraints, to discount the importance of the Arabs and their rights in his overall scheme of what was just. The Morrison-Grady plan, he told more than one person, was the solution to the Palestine problem that he considered most fair. Yet he backed away from this plan (which rejected partition and spelled doom for a Jewish state) because it was politically unsupportable in the United States. Clearly, to do what was "right" was a difficult task.

One option other than a Jewish state that might have been available to displaced European Jews, as it had been to their persecuted brethren in earlier years, was immigration to the United States. Quotas, however, restricted Jewish immigration, and the president knew that the reaction in this country if he attempted to change those quotas would be divisive. One poll taken in January 1946 indicated that only 5 per cent of those who responded favored increased immigration from Europe. Another poll taken in 1946 found that only 43 per cent favored allowing Poles, Jews, and other displaced persons to enter the United States.   "I think there would be terrific resistance if we attempted at this time to bring even a small portion [of displaced European Jews] into our own country beyond the present quota limitations," David Niles wrote the president in May 1946. "I don't see how we can ask other countries [i.e., outside the Arab world] to do what we ourselves are unable to do." These observations imply that Arab views could be discounted; they also suggest that there was more than a grain of truth to Bevin's subsequent accusation that "The average citizen does not want them [i.e., Jewish immigrants] in the United States and salves his conscience by advocating their admission to Palestine."

The president, meanwhile, found it easier to discount Arab opposition to U.S. policy in the Middle East than to confront bigotry and anti-Semitism in the United States. This explains, perhaps, why his efforts in opening up immigration quotas were limited and why he did not push Congress to expand quotas for refugees. Only in 1947 did the White House begin a concerted campaign to produce extensive refugee settlement in the United States, and by June 1948 only 41,379 refugees (who were not all Jewish) had entered the United States under the president's executive order.

If the president was sensitive to domestic prejudice and more cognizant of the imperatives of Zionism than the Department of State, he remained insensitive to Arab concerns about the introduction of 100,000 Jews to Palestine and, because of domestic pressures, he refused to share British responsibility for the larger problem of finding a fair solution to the Palestine question. He ignored the principle of self-determination which, presumably, he did not feel applied to the Arabs of Palestine and endorsed (but would not enforce) a partition plan that responded to Jewish needs but was manifestly unfair to the Arabs of Palestine.[59]

President Truman's support for partition gave international recognition to the Jewish claim of sovereignty in Palestine; his *de facto* recognition of Israel gave the state international legitimacy and

---

[59]John Morton Blum, ed, *The Price of Vision: The Diary of Henry A. Wallace, 1942-1946*, (Boston: Houghton Mifflin, 1973), p. 407; unpublished MS, Henry Grady Papers, Truman Library; Bain, *The March to Zion* pp. xv, 53, 58-60, 88-91, 162, 197-8, 202; Wilson, *Decision on Palestine*, pp. 137, 155; Cohen, *Palestine and the Great Powers, 1945-1948*, p. 395; May 27, 1946 memo from David Niles to President Truman, reprinted in Abram L. Sachar, *Redemption of the Unwanted: From the Liberation of the Death Camps to the Founding of Israel* (New York: St. Martin's, 1983), pp. 316-18; Edward Stettinius, Jr., *Roosevelt and the Russians: The Yalta Conference* (Garden City, N.Y.: Doubleday, 1949), pp. 289-290; and Wilson, pp. 50-56. For further discussion on immigration issues, see also: Grose, *Israel in the Mind of America*, pp. 32-33, 120, 200-210, 338; Cohen, pp. 14-15, 101-102, 118-19, 393; Sykes, *Crossroads to Israel*, pp. 377-380; Truman, *Years of Trial and Hope*, pp. 133-34. On the question of the fairness of partition see Wilson, pp. 112-13 and 128, who notes that Jews were given 53% of the land area of Palestine although they owned only 7% of the land and constituted only one-third of the population.

began the special relationship between the United States and Israel. It should be pointed out, however, that it was the Jews themselves, not Truman, who were responsible for bringing Israel into being. Partition probably would have come about even without his support. The result was also bound to reflect the relative strength of the parties involved. The United States does share responsibility, however, for the development of a situation that contributed to the plight of the Palestinian people, and the president bears some responsibility for never attempting to initiate a long-term solution to the problem of Palestine. Subject to the dichotomous views of his bureaucracy and lacking the substantive knowledge to judge their validity, he pursued policies that only put off or mitigated problems he did not understand and for which he had no solution.[60]

If the solid reputation that President Truman enjoys among most historians today can be attributed in part to the Truman Doctrine and the policies that supported containment of the Soviet Union in the Near East during the early years of the Cold War, it is also true, as one historian has noted, that his reputation "must stand on spheres other than Palestine."[61] The Palestine problem, it must be acknowledged, provided him with little room for maneuver. While the plight of Europe's surviving Jews clearly necessitated heroic efforts on the part of the world community, the world's reluctance to accommodate them, and the survivors' need for redemption from the traumas of the Holocaust, ultimately pointed to a solution that could be effected only at the expense of the Arab majority in Palestine and against the wishes of the Arab world. Rectifying one injustice by helping to perpetrate another, American policy supported the creation of a Jewish state while helping to sow the seeds of future conflict.

"The price for treating the Arab view-point as unimportant," Alan Bullock has observed of British policy during the Mandate, "has continued to be paid long after the British have left the Middle East." [62]

---

[60]Ganin, *Truman, American Jewry, and Israel*, pp. 146, 188-89; Donovan, *Conflict and Crisis*, p. 386; Wilson, *Decision on Palestine*, p. 148; Cohen, *Palestine and the Great Powers, 1945-1948*, pp. 44-45, 389, 393; Grose, *Israel in the Mind of America*, p. 192. See also n. 53 earlier in this book.

[61]Cohen, *Palestine and the Great Powers, 1945-1948*, p. 389.

[62]Bullock, *Ernest Bevin*, p. 169.

The United States, needless to say, is one of those still paying that price, a good part of which was set by the 1948 war. The Palestine refugee problem, which was not anticipated, and which American officials assumed would be resolved in a year or two, proved unresponsive to economic approaches. Failure to address it in any meaningful way also was to prove an important factor in each of the subsequent Arab-Israeli wars.

It is not necessary to chronicle here the complex histories of the Arab-Israeli wars or the various civil wars in Jordan and Lebanon that have taken place over the last 37 years. Volumes have been written about those wars, about the important part played by the unresolved Palestinian problem in precipitating them, and about various efforts (guided by carefully worded resolutions) to address (or ignore) at least a part of that problem. In time, as we have seen, the need of Palestinians for a homeland would be recognized by many as parallel to that of the Jews, and the sympathies of the United Nations, its ranks tripled by nations of the emerging Third World, would be profoundly altered.

The focus here is more narrow: to underscore increasing United States interest in and concern for the Palestine problem as the Palestinian nationalist movement, impinging on the world's conscience in the wake of the 1967 war, began to gather momentum. It was in that war that the Israelis occupied not only the Sinai and the Golan, but the West Bank (including East Jerusalem) and Gaza Strip as well, once again precipitating an exodus of Palestinian refugees into the neighboring Arab states where many turned from Gamal Abdel Nasser to themselves for a solution to their plight. Following their enormous losses during the Jordan civil war of 1970-71, and the subsequent resurrection in Lebanon of the P.L.O. (recognized in the aftermath of the October 1973 War by the 1974 Rabat Summit decision that designated the P.L.O. as "the sole legitimate spokesman of the Palestinian people"), Secretary of State Kissinger would approve a statement declaring the Palestine problem to be, in many ways, the "heart" of the Arab-Israeli conflict. Subsequently, when confronted by a hostile Israeli reaction, he would dismiss the statement he reportedly had cleared with President Ford as an "academic and theoretical exercise." The Palestinian movement, however, could not be so easily dismissed.[63]

---

[63]See, for example, Kennet Love, *Suez: The Twice-Fought War* (New York: McGraw-Hill, 1969), pp. 23 ff.; Donald Neff,

World opinion, prodded by the oil embargo, would gradually induce the United States first to broaden its conceptions of both American and Israæli security interests and then to include in those conceptions a constructive response to the needs of the Palestinians.   American officials would increasingly recognize that the necessity of addressing the concerns of *both* Israælis and Palestinians, and of mediating their conflict, was dictated not only by international pressures, but by the historical consequences of continuing to ignore the Palestinian problem. A moral imperative to address the concerns of both peoples, some believed, derived from a related set of historical responsibilities: for contributing to the plight of the Jews by failing to change U.S. immigration laws; for endorsing a solution to the Jewish problem that encouraged Jewish immigration to Palestine (where the United States incurred a responsibility for their welfare); and, finally, for contributing to the plight of the Palestinians who, as a result, found their homeland occupied and many of their brethren dispossessed. Recognition of these responsibilities and a willingness to contribute to the rectification of some (but not all) historical injustices, it was believed, would help to restore Palestinian dignity, ensure Israæli security, and so meliorate the conflict between Arab and Jew. This perception of the Palestinian problem, at least in part, would inform the policies of the Carter Administration which, though it failed in its efforts, was the first American administration to undertake on a presidential level an initiative that attempted to address the Palestinian problem in all of its aspects.

Warriors at Suez: Eisenhower Takes America into the Middle East (New York: Linden Press/Simon & Schuster, 1981), pp. 29-47; Walter Laqueur, *The Road to War: The Origins and Aftermath of the Arab-Israæli Conflict, 1967-8* (London: Pelican, 1968, 1969), p. 74; Donald Neff, *Warriors for Jerusalem: The Six Days that Changed the Middle East* (New York: Simon & Schuster, 1984); William Quandt, *Decade of Decisions: American Policy Toward the Arab-Israæli Conflict, 1967-1976* (Berkeley: University of California Press, 1977), pp. 278-279; Edward Sheehan, *The Arabs, Israælis, and Kissinger: A Secret History of American Diplomacy in the Middle East* (New York: Reader's Digest Press, 1974), pp. 212-213; John Cooley, *Green March, Black September*; Kamal S. Salibi, *Cross Roads to Civil War: Lebanon, 1958-1976* (Delmar, N.Y.: Caravan, 1976); Walid Khalidi, *Conflict and Violence in Lebanon;* David Gordon, *Lebanon: The Fragmented Nation*; Itamar Rabinovich, *The War For Lebanon, 1970-1983*, Ze'ev Schiff and Ehud Ya'ari, *Israæl's Lebanon War* (New York: Simon & Schuster, 1984).

After grappling with the issue for some time, the Carter administration eventually sought to define a process that would temporarily circumvent the complex issue of sovereignty over the occupied territories. This approach would have permitted the Palestinian Arabs political self-expression, while making it possible for the Israelis to maintain a presence that safeguarded their security and fulfilled what they regarded as their right to be there. Under the Camp David Accords, Israel and Egypt agreed to provide "full autonomy" to the inhabitants of the West Bank and Gaza. Full autonomy was to be exercised through a freely elected self-governing authority during a five-year transitional period, with the status of the West Bank and Gaza and its relationship with its neighbors to be decided at the end of the five-year period.[64]

President Carter apparently believed that the ambiguous formulation of "autonomy" for the Palestinians (which was debated extensively but never successfully defined) would allow for eventual agreement. In time, he hoped, agreement on autonomy would make it possible for Israelis and Palestinians to demonstrate their ability to live in peace and would lead to a solution that fulfilled the legitimate objectives of both.[65]

Prime Minister Begin's goals appear to have been both different and more limited: a separate peace with Egypt and, along with rejection of the concept of a Palestinian state, as free a hand as possible for Israel in the occupied territories. From a Palestinian perspective, "full autonomy" was a euphemism for Israeli control, which was never acceptable. From the Israeli government's perspective, "full autonomy" clearly meant something less than "sovereignty," and it was to be exercised by the "inhabitants" of that land over themselves—not over the land itself. Begin subsequently reserved the right to assert Israel's claim of sovereignty to all of the West Bank in negotiations on its final status, and asserted that he would do so. His settlement policies, which his

---

[64] Harold Saunders, *The Middle East Problem in the 1980s* (Washington, D.C.: American Enterprise Institute, 1981), pp. 40-41; the Camp David Accords can be found in Congressional Quarterly, *Middle East: US Policy, Israel, Oil and the Arabs*, 4th ed. (Washington, D.C.: Congressional Quarterly, 1979).

[65] Carter, *Keeping Faith*, p. 335, 428.

Likud successors continue to support, suggest that at least his party intends to keep his pledge.[66]

Israel's early rejection of the Reagan Plan of September 1, 1982 supports this assessment of the Likud's intentions. The Reagan Plan asserts that peace cannot be achieved on the basis of Israeli sovereignty over the West Bank and Gaza, but must be based on U.N. Resolution 242's formula of territory for peace. The plan opposes the creation of a Palestinian state on the West Bank and Gaza, and instead asserts its

---

[66]From remarks made at Duke University by Yochanan Ramati, chairman of the foreign policy committee of the Leam Wing of the Likud Party, on a visit to Durham, NC, Nov. 1982; "Text of Israel's Communique on the Reagan Plan," *New York Times*, Sept. 3, 1982; Trudy Rubin, *Christian Science Monitor*, Sept. 2-3, 1982. In his memoirs, Carter notes of his discussions with Begin on Sept. 16, 1978:

> On the West Bank settlements we finally worked out language that was satisfactory: that no new Israeli settlements would be established after the signing of the Framework for Peace, and that the issue of additional settlements would be resolved by the parties during negotiations. This would be stated in a letter, to be made public, from Begin to me. (Begin later denied that he had agreed to this, and claimed that he had promised to stop building settlements only for a three-month period. My notes are clear—that the settlement freeze would continue until all negotiations were completed—and Cy Vance confirms my interpretation of what we decided....)

Carter, *Keeping Faith*, p. 397. Also see Vance, *Hard Choices*, pp. 225-228, Moshe Dayan, *Breakthrough: A Personal Account of the Egypt-Israel Peace Negotiations* (New York: Knopf, 1981), pp. 181-188, and the differing interpretations of Sol Linowitz and Philip Geylin, *International Herald Tribune*, June 18-19, 1983. Begin's reaction to President Reagan's request for an immediate adoption of a freeze on settlements is also clear. On the following day, Begin denied the idea of a freeze. Three days after Reagan's speech, Israel approved plans for seven new settlements, while rumors about more were rife. On Dec. 8, 1982, *Ha'aretz* reported that the Likud intended to build 35 new settlements in the West Bank in the coming year.

preference for self-government by the Palestinians in association with Jordan, with the extent of Israeli withdrawal determined by the quality of peace offered in return.[67]

Prime Minister Begin's reaction was predictable. Rabbi Arthur Hertzberg, former President of the American Jewish Congress, put it succinctly:

> The new American initiative has now made it clear, even to those who have preferred not to see, that if the forces of heavenly angels themselves were deployed to protect an Israel that had lost sovereignty over the West Bank, Menachem Begin would nonetheless stand before God and demand that he keep his promise to return the whole of their homeland to the Jews.

Yitzhak Shamir, who was foreign minister at the time, was subsequently prime minister, and is again foreign minister in the national unity government, has insisted that Israel would never part with "Judea" and "Samaria" and that if the Reagan Plan had been put forward as the American position at the time of Camp David, Israel would not have signed the accords. This assertion, while undoubtedly correct, is misleading. As President Carter notes in his memoirs, Prime Minister Begin at Camp David rejected U.N. Security Council Resolution 242's stipulation that the acquisition of territory by war was inadmissible; instead, Begin argued that the 1967 war was a defensive act which gave Israel the right to keep and occupy lands taken in its own defense. Neither the United States nor Egypt accepted Israel's position or interpretation. If the ambiguous formulation on autonomy had been defined according to Israeli desires, neither Sadat nor Carter would have signed the accords. What they did sign, and what Begin signed, was a document sufficiently flexible to allow for compromise should good faith prevail. President Carter, meanwhile, reserved the right to put forward compromise proposals. Over two years after the

---

[67]The text is in the *New York Times*, Sept. 2, 1982; see also "Text of Talking Points Sent to Begin by President," *New York Times*, Sept. 9, 1982, for clarification of the plan; and two public addresses by George Shultz: "President Reagan's Middle East Peace Initiative," Sept. 10, 1982, U.S. Department of State, Bureau of Public Affairs, *Current Policy* No. 418, and "The Quest for Peace," Sept. 12, 1982, *Current Policy* No. 419.

date set as a goal for establishment of a self-governing authority for the West Bank and Gaza, no agreement had been reached in the autonomy talks; good faith had not prevailed.

The Reagan Plan, drawn up in response to these developments, was consistent with the guidelines followed by Carter in the course of the negotiations at Camp David. Differences of interpretation raise the question of whether or not it is in Israel's best interests to accept the Reagan Plan as a basis for negotiations.[68] Many Israelis, particularly those who support the Labor Party, oppose the Likud's determination to retain sovereignty over all of the occupied territories. They also share a number of the concerns voiced by proponents of a Palestinian state. They have serious problems, however, with the idea of sovereignty for the Palestinians—unless the concept is markedly qualified by safeguards that are essential to Israel's security. These safeguards, they reason, would be a fair exchange for the risks Israel would have to take were it to support "full autonomy" for the Palestinians. For this reason, they look to proposals that modify sovereignty and that include some combination of self- and shared-rule between a Palestinian entity, Jordan, and Israel.[69]

---

[68]Hertzberg, *New York Review of Books*, Oct. 21, 1982; David Shipler, *New York Times*, Sept. 9, 1982; "Israeli Authorities in Sharp Opposition to Reagan Proposals," *Washington Post*, Sept. 2, 1982; Carter, *Keeping Faith*, pp. 333, 354, 367, and 386. President Carter is convinced that the Reagan Plan is absolutely compatible with the Camp David Agreements. See Shultz, "President Reagan's Middle East Peace Initiative"; Secretary of State Shultz has clearly stated the administration's position that the interests of the Palestinians and Israelis are not mutually exclusive. In a speech to the UN, he observed that the Palestinian claim to a place with which they could identify was undeniable; he also noted that it was only possible for them to achieve their legitimate rights in a context which gave to Israel what it had a right to demand: "to exist and to exist in peace and security." For the text, see the *New York Times*, October 1, 1982, p. A 10. Howard Sachar has observed that Reagan has transcended but not transgressed the negotiations at Camp David. Howard Sachar, *Washington Post*, September 2, 1982.

[69]For the Labor Party's response to the Reagan Plan and Shimon Peres's characterization of it as a basis for dialogue, see *New York Times*, Sept. 3, 1982. For the tentatively favorable

Meanwhile, the vociferous reactions of Begin, Shamir, and the Likud coalition to the Reagan Plan—which calls for Palestinian autonomy in association with Jordan—make it obvious that espousal of a Palestinian state by the United States, however desirable in terms of some abstract principle of justice, and however consistent it might be with the principles of self-determination of peoples codified in the United Nations Charter, is not likely to lead to it. None of the main political parties in Israel would support creation of a Palestinian state. The concept does not have any substantial support in the United States, where no serious presidential candidate was prepared to endorse it during the 1984 election year. Such a proposal would cause grave anxieties among Israelis, damage any possibility of a constructive alternative to the Israeli government's current policies on the Palestinian question, and undermine the American role as mediator and treaty guarantor.

Clearly, a *modus vivendi* is required. A number of Israelis who oppose a Palestinian state, and many Arabs who might prefer one, regard the Reagan Plan as a constructive response to this situation. They see such an approach as a pragmatic alternative that deserves careful attention. The problem that they have had with the Reagan Plan is not so much with its proposals as with the administration's lack of political will in attempting to implement them.[70]

Despite events since the Reagan Plan was announced, peace is not unattainable. Rather, the fundamental problem is a lack of political will—on the part of the Israelis to compromise on the question of

---

responses of AIPAC and B'nai B'rith, see the articles by Bernard Gwertzman, *New York Times*, Sept.7.9, 1982; see also "Dissent & Israel: An Exchange," *New York Review of Books*, Nov. 18, 1983, pp.73-77.

[70] For discussion of Labor Party attitudes: Yigal Allon, "Israel: The Case for Defensible Borders," *Foreign Affairs* 55 (Oct. 1976). pp. 38-53; Abba Eban, "Camp David: The Unfinished Business," *Foreign Affairs* 57 (Winter 1978/79), pp.343-354; Shimon Peres, "A Strategy for Peace in the Middle East," *Foreign Affairs* 58 (Spring 1980), pp.887-901. Mark Bruzonsky's thoughtful article, "America's Palestinian Predicament: Fallacies and Possibilities," *International Security* 7 (Summer 1982), pp.93-110, analyzes the semantic confusion surrounding solutions to the Palestinian question.

territory and Palestinian rights, on the part of the Palestinians to recognize and negotiate with Israel, and on the part of the United States to use its influence to facilitate a process of mutual accommodation that must take place if there is to be a peaceful settlement. Concerned institutions and individuals, such as those who collaborated on the Brookings Report in 1975, have isolated problems that need to be addressed. They have attempted to define principles that would govern a settlement and to explore the contents of a possible agreement. In the course of their endeavors they have examined the importance of safeguards, demilitarized zones, great power guarantees, and various forms of assistance in reinforcing commitments. In an effort to avoid pressures for one-sided implementation of any agreement, they have considered carefully the role of stages in the process of implementation, and reflected on the linkages between stages of withdrawal from occupied territory and manifestations of peaceful intent. To preclude military actions, they have looked hard at the interposition of force, limitations on military equipment, the creation of physical barriers, and zones of separation and denial. Their writings lead one to believe that practical implementation of a solution is not impossible and that it is not even the main problem. The most difficult problem, recent history suggests, is mustering the political will necessary to set the peace process in motion and encourage its realization.[71]

The key to thinking about a constructive solution to the Palestinian question is to avoid becoming immobilized by categorical positions and semantics, and to support mechanisms that will permit the Palestinians to have as much real authority as possible over themselves, the West Bank and Gaza, and their resources, while simultaneously making it possible for the Israelis to avoid the security risks that they believe would be inherent in an independent, sovereign Palestinian state.

---

[71]For the Brookings Report, see "Toward Peace in the Middle East," *Report of a Study Group* (Washington, D.C.: Brookings Institution, 1975). Its members included Zbigniew Brzezinski, Nadav Safran, and William Quandt, whose book *Decade of Decisions: American Policy Toward the Arab-Israeli Conflict, 1967-1976* (Berkeley: University of California Press, 1977) is particularly thoughtful.

III

THE PALESTINIAN PROBLEM
AND OTHER U.S. INTERESTS
IN THE MIDDLE EAST

If the task of reconciling Palestinian and Isræli differences is so difficult, why, one might ask, aside from an important moral obligation to both parties incurred in the course of the last century, does the United States continue to attempt it? Part of the answer lies in the connection between the Palestinian question and other U.S. interests in the Middle East—a connection which has been instrumental in motivating repeated attempts by recent American officials (from Secretaries of State Rogers and Kissinger to Secretary of State Shultz) to resolve the conflict.

The options that confront U.S. officials as they look down the road at U.S.-Isræli relations are disconcerting. As Isræl's retention of the occupied territories becomes increasingly unacceptable to the Palestinians who live there, Isræl increasingly will be forced to intensify security measures, progressively weakening its political and moral position in international fora. In time, increased tensions and longstanding hostilities in the region, fueled by the resources of the Arab world and on occasion by the Soviet Union, undoubtedly will force Isræl to increase its requests for U.S. security assistance, as it did in 1973.

If the U.S fails to meet Isræli security requests, Isrælis would feel increasingly vulnerable. They would also be more likely to strike preemptively at their foes, as they did in 1967, possibly involving themselves in wars that could escalate out of control. As the October 1973 War made clear, and as Isræli-Syrian confrontations over Lebanon suggest, Isræli policies have the potential for involving the United States in serious—and possibly nuclear—confrontations with the Soviet Union as well.

If the United States meets Isræli security requests, on the other hand, the U.S.-Isræli relationship will reinforce Arab and Muslim perceptions that American assistance is the prime reason why Isræl is able to deny Palestinians their "legitimate rights." These perceptions, in turn, which aggravate the radical Arab regimes and have long separated them from the United States, will generate growing internal and external pressures on conservative regimes to distance themselves from the United States.

Regime responses to such pressures are conditioned by the complex trade-offs that are normally examined under such circumstances. Pressures to distance themselves from the United States are weighed against a recognition of the many ways in which the U.S. serves as a deterrent to Soviet or lesser (i.e., Iranian) intimidation. Nonetheless, since the Palestinian cause is an Arab cause, Arab regimes cannot ignore the fact that U.S. and Isræli policies toward the Palestinians constitute a profound insult to their dignity as Arabs. Hundreds of thousands of Palestinians live throughout the Gulf, often occupying important administrative, civil, commercial, educational, journalistic and political positions. One quarter of Kuwait's population, for example, is Palestinian. However cynical some of these regimes may have been about the Palestinian question, and however badly they may have treated the Palestinians themselves, the common bond between them cannot be ignored, particularly when it is solidified by common outrage over Isræli policies and apparent support for those policies by the United States.

The visceral responses of many Arabs to what they perceive as a lack of respect for the legitimate concerns of the Arab world should not be discounted. Regardless of what Arabs do to each other, their perceptions of what non-Arabs do to them contribute to a reservoir of anger that erodes what otherwise might be a far more favorable attitude toward the policies of the United States. An example of this phenomenon is the Arab attitude toward U.S. alarm at the Soviet invasion of Afghanistan. Many Arabs, while profoundly disturbed by events in Afghanistan, saw Isræli occupation of the West Bank and Gaza as a greater threat to the Arab world than the Soviet occupation of Afghanistan. They gave Isræl's policies on the West Bank more than equal time in international fora, such as the Islamic Conference or the Non Aligned Movement, complicating U.S. attempts to marshall world opinion against Soviet actions in Afghanistan.

In addition to complicating U.S. relations with friendly Arab regimes and inhibiting their receptivity to American concerns about larger security issues, the continued stalemate of the Palestinian question and the imperatives that flow from it could create serious problems for the United States. Such problems are matters of degree. The Saudis, for example, could find it increasingly difficult to associate themselves with U.S. policies and interests. To the extent that the Palestinian question is not addressed, criticism of the royal family's "irresponsible" use of the national patrimony (oil) to subsidize indirectly (through the United States) Zionist aspirations in the West Bank and Jerusalem is likely to challenge the House of Saud's Islamic and Arab credentials and directly affect its legitimacy.[72] Israeli actions such as the bombing of Iraq's newly constructed nuclear reactor in June 1981, or the invasion of Lebanon in June 1982, reinforce perceptions of the threat posed by Israel and the risks associated with too close a relationship with its primary ally the United States. Recognizing these threats to its legitimacy, the House of Saud might well consider reducing its ties with the United States, expanding its ties with Western Europe and Japan, and one day normalizing its relations with the Soviet Union.[73] U.S. influence in the region would diminish, Israel and the

---

[72]See Bruce Kuniholm, "What the Saudis Really Want: A Primer for the Reagan Administration," *Orbis* 25 (Spring 1981), pp. 107-121. For a discussion of the spiritual and psychic needs that have stimulated the recent quest for a return to the Islamic ethos, see R. Hrair Dekmejian, "The Anatomy of Islamic Revival: Legitimacy Crisis, Ethnic Conflict and the Search for Islamic Alternatives," *Middle East Journal* 34 (Winter 1980), pp. 1-12.

[73]For a former State Department intelligence analyst's perception of Saudi attempts to distance themselves from the United States, see Malcolm Peck, *Christian Science Monitor*, Aug. 12, 1983, who notes that the Saudis "view the Arab-Israeli conflict as the main cause of Arab radicalism and divisiveness and, therefore, as the principal threat to their security." As a consequence of the belief that the United States is unwilling or unable to compel Israeli acceptance of American ideas, many want a less close alignment with the United States. For one report of the "thaw" between the Soviet Union and Saudi Arabia, see Dusko Doder, *International Herald Tribune*, June 7, 1983.

United States would be isolated, and U.S. interests and capabilities to counter Soviet intimidation of regional states would suffer.

Other Gulf states, meanwhile, could turn increasingly to Western European markets for their armament needs and to the European Community (E.C.) and Japan to meet their technological, infrastructural, and business requirements. In isolation, these developments would pose few problems. But most of the Gulf states, as previously mentioned, have sizable Palestinian populations; they are also responsive to Palestinian concerns and fear Arab radicalism, which the Palestinian problem has consistently provoked and which polarization of the Palestinian national movement by Syria may well exacerbate. As a result, they could insist on a more pro-Palestinian line from the E.C. as a *quid pro quo* for their business or their oil. If and when the current oil glut diminishes, and as the Gulf states gain control of oil deliveries "downstream," the oil weapon—directed against U.S. policies toward Israel—could exacerbate U.S.-European differences and directly undermine NATO.[74]

What is remarkable about some of these speculations is not that there is a reasonable basis for them, but that the United States, not the Soviet Union, could set them in motion; and the Soviet Union, not the United States, would benefit from them. Israel, in some abstract sense, may constitute a strategic asset in the region because of its military capability and its apparent reliability, but it also constitutes a strategic liability. The close association between Israel and the U.S., to the extent that it leads the United States to ignore the Palestinian problem, to disregard other U.S. interests and to alienate most of the states within the region, has the clear potential for undermining regimes that cooperate with the United States, thereby creating massive inroads for Soviet influence. This argument has been voiced since 1948, and it has only partially been realized. Developments of the last decade and a half, however, beginning with the advent of the Palestinian national movement in the wake of the 1967 war, coupled with Britain's withdrawal from the Gulf in 1968-71, and followed by the increased leverage over oil prices exercised by the Arab states after the 1973 war, make it more likely than before. The financial power of the Gulf states to address regional concerns is a mixed blessing in that it also makes

[74]See discussion of this possibility in *Wall Street Journal*, Apr. 8, 1981.

them increasingly vulnerable to the charge that they have done nothing to resolve those concerns—and in fact have helped *prevent* their resolution. All that is necessary to set in motion the process described above is continued inactivity on the Palestinian question in conjunction with the development of serious internal difficulties within one of the Gulf states closely associated with the United States. Neither radical nor more "democratic" regimes are likely to be more favorably disposed toward Israel. When supported by the Soviet Union, they would pose an even greater threat to U.S. interests than before.

IV

WHAT IS TO BE DONE?

If one can accept the logic of the arguments discussed above, it follows that the American government, in the aftermath of Israel's withdrawal from Lebanon, has basically three options: letting things drift, trying again to revitalize the peace process, or pursuing an alternative strategy for addressing the Palestinian question in all its aspects. If the United States chooses to let things drift, it will leave the initiative to others; in such circumstances, it will have little option but to respond to events precipitated either by Palestinian terrorism (the weapon of the weak) or by Israeli policies such as the invasion of Lebanon and *de facto* annexation of the West Bank.

If the United States chooses to confront the Arab-Israeli conflict, on the other hand, and to address the Palestinian question, whether through pursuit of the Camp David framework and the Reagan Plan or some alternative, it must, in part, be able to count on Arab willingness to negotiate directly with Israel. As former U.S. Ambassador Robert Neumann has pointed out, "the U.S. government simply does not have the political capability to respond positively to any Arab peace overture short of an offer of direct negotiations between the parties concerned." The kind of Arab commitment it would take was evidenced by President Anwar Sadat's willingness to go to Jerusalem in November 1977.

For any Arab regime, the risks involved are enormous. They include losing legitimacy within the Arab world and, as the example of Sadat makes clear, losing one's life as well. As a result, one of the key variables is the *quid pro quo* that the United States can offer. Arab leaders recognize the enormous influence that the United States has over Israel; like Sadat, they believe it to be even greater than history warrants. At the same time, they harbor doubts that the United States can "deliver" on such divisive matters as Israeli settlement policies on the West Bank, and consequently are unwilling to legitimate the Israeli government through negotiation without a clear *quid pro quo*. Arab leaders are also relatively immune to the leverage—primarily security assistance—that the U.S. possesses. Internal threats to security, which center around the challenge to legitimacy, are generally given priority over regional, military threats. Such priorities make the Arab states cautious about the kinds of security assistance the United States can provide.

Whether the kind of commitment to negotiate evidenced earlier by Sadat will present itself again under Jordan's King Hussein depends in part on the Arabs themselves. It depends on Hussein's and Arafat's courage in making some difficult choices. It also depends on the Reagan administration's willingness not only to come to terms with the Palestinian movement, but to mediate the problem of mutual recognition of national rights. Another important variable is the ability of the United States to draw Syria into the peace process, which undoubtedly relates to the prospects of the Golan being returned to Syria. Assad's capacity to prevent the May 17, 1983 agreement between Israel and Lebanon, to frustrate both U.S. and Israeli policies in Lebanon, and to split the P.L.O., together underscore his ability, if his interests are not met, to cut the legs out from under Hussein and Arafat. A warning to this effect was probably issued through the assassination in December 1984 of Fahd Kawasmeh, a key moderate on the P.L.O. Executive Committee, whose death appeared to be a clear message to the P.L.O.; similar messages to the Jordanians have probably been issued through the assassination of Jordanian diplomats in Bucharest and Ankara, as well as attacks on Jordan's national airline, Alia, and on the Jordanian embassy in Rome.[75]

----

[75]For the quote from Neumann, see "Middle East: America's Next Steps," pp. 106-122. At present, it is Hussein's role that is central. For a recent U.S. assertion that the territories-for-peace assumption of the Reagan Plan applies to all Israeli fronts including the Golan Heights, see Don Oberdorfer, *Washington Post*, Feb. 17, 1985. For interpretation of the assassinations, see Jonathan Randal, *Washington Post*, January 17, 1985, and Christopher Dickey, *Washington Post*, August 6, 1985. For Assad's goals, see Milton Viorst, *Christian Science Monitor*, August 7, 1985. Henry Kissinger has written that, "[b]efore launching a new set of negotiations, an exploration of Syrian views would seem essential. And, if these views are rejected,

Hussein's commitment to negotiate, finally, depends on Israeli policies toward the West Bank. Israel's annexationist policies toward the occupied territories, more than any other problem, Carter administration officials believed, kept the United States from facilitating a process of mutual accommodation between the Israelis and Palestinians.[76] If this is still so and one accepts the argument that the practical problems of peace are not insurmountable, the crucial question concerns the extent to which the United States can exercise the political will necessary to set the peace process in motion. Because massive U.S. assistance to Israel to a great extent determines the constraints on Israeli policies, and because Israeli policies have the potential not only to work against U.S. interests in the Middle East, but to draw the United States into a global confrontation with the Soviet Union as well, it is only reasonable that the American government, in addressing the Arab-Israeli conflict (and providing that the Palestinians are able and prepared to negotiate), consider carefully how and to what degree it can constructively influence Israel to cooperate in the peace process on the basis of mutual recognition of national rights. While the problem was not examined seriously during the 1984 election year, the second Reagan administration now has the opportunity to do so relatively free from domestic political pressures.

---

the United States must be willing to devote the energy and resources to prevail in the resulting showdown. If the United States is not to demoralize its allies and undermine irretrievably the position of its Arab friends, it must clearly define its objectives before it commits itself." *Washington Post*, July 31, 1985. The U.S. experience in Lebanon, of course, illustrates the consequences of ignoring the Syrian factor.

[76]For Egyptian and American officials' assessments of Israel's annexation policies, see Vance, *Hard Choices*, pp. 237, 254. Henry Kissinger and Harold Saunders have both said that the U.S. cannot accept annexation of the West Bank. See Daniel Southerland, *Christian Science Monitor*, Sept. 1, 1983.

V

CARROTS OR STICKS? THE QUESTION OF U.S. INFLUENCE OVER ISRAEL

A former member of the National Security Council staff, William Quandt, observed a few years ago that during their terms in the White House, Presidents Nixon and Ford each subscribed to both the following views at different times:

> If Israel is to feel sufficiently secure to make the territorial concessions necessary to gain Arab acceptance of the terms of a peace agreement, she must continue to receive large quantities of American military and economic aid.
>
> If Israel feels too strong and self-confident, she will not see the need for any change in the *status quo*. United States aid must therefore be withheld as a form of pressure.[77]

Clearly, while recognizing the complexities and importance of other factors, both presidents sought some combination of carrot and stick that would cause Israel to take the steps necessary for peace. Since the Nixon and Ford administrations, the search for an appropriate combination of inducements and pressures to influence Israeli policies has been central to the concerns of the Carter and Reagan administrations as well.

Most recently, Israel's war in Lebanon, its destruction of a sizable portion of the P.L.O.'s military infrastructure, and its continuing annexation of the West Bank, together have raised once again the question of U.S. influence over Israel. Whether the United States can or will influence Israel to rely less on its armed forces and to take the risks

---

[77]Quandt, *Decade of Decisions*, p. 321.

necessary for peace remains to be seen. The Arab states, it has been noted, must be prepared to reciprocate and the conditions must be propitious. King Hussein's recent peace initiatives and renewed relations with Egypt suggest that Jordan's cautious monarch may be ready to take such risks. Conditions are also favorable: Israel is withdrawing from Lebanon and is led (at least until Shimon Peres's 25-month term expires in 1986) by a prime minister who is far more receptive to compromise than his recent predecessors; Arab leaders in Egypt, Saudi Arabia and Iraq have indicated support for Hussein's initiatives; the divided P.L.O. has few options and its chairman may be prepared to be more realistic than before about his course of action; Syria, having regrouped since its losses during the 1982 war, is now in a position to negotiate, and Soviet hints suggest a receptivity even on their part. Because the United States once more has the opportunity to play a constructive role in the search for an elusive peace, and because Israeli policies on the West Bank may soon preclude the possibility of a *modus vivendi* between Israelis and Palestinians, the question of America's role in the peace process and American influence over Israel, which has been of primary concern to all recent administrations, continues to be the subject of discussion.

A recent study that has taken a close look at the role played by mediators in the Arab-Israeli conflict argues that the mediator's ability to induce the various parties to make concessions and compromises is sensitive to situational pressures and derives from material resources at the mediator's disposal. It also finds that concessions are less likely on issues affecting "core values," while agreements are more difficult to achieve to the extent that they are comprehensive in scope.[78]

Arguing that the mediator's role depends on the parties' acceptance of the mediator, the author of the study, Saadia Touval, views the mediator's ability to apply pressure as constrained. Material resources have enabled the mediator to exert only limited pressure on the parties; incentives and compensation for concessions are more important than pressures, and are most effective when both sides benefit—especially if

---

[78] Saadia Touval, *The Peace Brokers: Mediators in the Arab-Israeli Conflict, 1948-1979* (Princeton,N.J.: Princeton University Press, 1982), pp. 309, 326-327, 330.

what is perceived as a zero-sum game is transformed into a positive-sum game.[79]

Touval does not discuss Israel's dependence on the United States—a dependence which on occasion, even when Israel opposes mediation, has given it little choice but to accept United States involvement. Clearly, this dependence diminishes the bargaining power that Touval attributes to Israel: the implied threat of withdrawing consent to the United States' playing a mediator's role.

Statistics cited earlier suggest that one cannot so easily dismiss the notion that there are circumstances under which the U.S. can withhold economic, financial, or military aid to Israel. Whether such a course is politically feasible is a moot point, but chances of success would certainly be more likely if the decision were strongly encouraged by the American president, if the president were able to convince both the Israeli and American people that the policies he was advocating were in Israel's interest (and did not threaten its security), and if he were able to demonstrate to the American public that continuation of aid at current levels gave the Israeli government the means to adversely affect U.S. interests in the Middle East.

Touval's main point suggests the desirability of a much less activist course of action. The root causes of the Arab-Israeli conflict, he argues, are too complex and deeply imbedded in national ideologies for a mediator to resolve. Resolution of the conflict requires not skillful mediation so much as a transformation of national values and ideologies. As a result, mediators should recognize their limitations, modify excessive aspirations, and work for "small" agreements that reduce the conflict, so contributing to a process that may eventually lead to mutual accommodation.[80]

Former Secretary of State Henry Kissinger's attitude toward the question of U.S. influence over Israel is similar to Touval's and deserves

---

[79]Touval, *The Peace Brokers*, pp. 15, 103, 326-327, 331. "The implied threat of withdrawing consent to the third party's playing a mediator's role is of course one of the important bargaining assets of parties *vis-a-vis* the mediator." Touval, p. 15.

[80]Touval, *The Peace Brokers*, p. 331.

brief elaboration. According to Kissinger, the key to U.S. policy in the Middle East in the early years of the Nixon Administration was to reduce the scope of adventurist Soviet policies. A military stalemate, in Kissinger's opinion, would not have strengthened the Soviet position (as the State Department argued); rather, it would have demonstrated that the Soviets were unable to deliver what the Arabs wanted because Israel, with American help, could withstand Arab military power. The U.S., in turn, could block all diplomatic activity until the Arabs were ready to reciprocate Israeli concessions. Under these circumstances, American pressure on Israel would have been counterproductive— encouraging Arab radicals and Soviet clients, precluding Israeli concessions, and driving Israel to extreme actions. A comprehensive approach, on the other hand, would have favored radicals by giving intransigent governments a veto over negotiations and providing the Soviets with room to maneuver. As a result, it was essential for Arab leaders to understand that a settlement could not be extorted from the United States, that peace could not be achieved *without* the U.S., and that only the U.S. could exert influence over Israel.[81]

When it comes to the question of how the U.S. could influence Israel, Kissinger is sensitive to the factors that affect the conduct of Israel's foreign policy. Israel's domestic politics, he argues, require that those responsible for national security prove to their colleagues that there is no alternative to a chosen course. Their tenacious, nitpicking, legalistic method of negotiation, he asserts, is founded on a premonition of potential disaster and stems from a knowledge of Israel's vulnerability in the Middle East as a whole—whatever the current military balance. These and other judgments explain his view of a comprehensive peace as destined to bog down in niggling detail, more yearned for than attainable. Even U.S. pressures, Kissinger insists, would not bring about the comprehensive peace desired by the Arab states. A failed effort, moreover, would alienate Israelis *and* Arabs (who would be supported by our European and Japanese allies), leaving the U.S. isolated. Israel, in turn, would be led to desperate measures or psychological collapse. Weighing the rewards of success against the

---

[81]Henry Kissinger, *White House Years* (Boston: Little, Brown, 1979), pp. 347, 356-357, 376-379, 559.

penalties of failure, Kissinger argues that achievable objectives must be set within the psychological capacities of the negotiating parties.[82]

The real problem in the Middle East that emerges from Kissinger's writing is one that is psychological: acquiring the confidence to negotiate. What may have given confidence to Sadat, Kissinger's memoirs suggest, were such factors as the achievement of "face," or the restoration of self-respect, honor, and dignity.[83] Israel, too, needed confidence, which is why the crucial issue of security, the reversal of the momentum of conflict by stages, and a predictable U.S. policy—unaccompanied by threatened pressures—are important to the Israelis. Kissinger's concern to maintain Israel's trust in the United States and his fear that desperation would make Israel more defiant led him on several occasions (in December 1973, May 1974, and August 1974) to oppose or deflect what he characterizes as Nixon's desire to use economic pressure on Israel.[84]

Kissinger recognizes that if Israel doesn't run risks, seeking instead to rest its existence on naked force, it will "consume its moral substance."[85] What he would do to encourage Israel to run such risks, however, is unclear. After the Israeli invasion of Lebanon, Kissinger in an interview with the *Economist* again addressed the problem, observing that Israeli incorporation of the West Bank and Gaza would either destroy the essence of the Jewish state (because of demographic factors), or, if Israel expells the Arabs, cause it to lose the moral support of its best friends.[86]

If this were to happen, Kissinger believes, Israel would not be able to withstand the crisis that would result. He is careful, however, about the implications of his analysis. Believing that Israeli self-confidence needs little if any encouragement, he argues that the U.S. should

---

[82]Henry Kissinger, *Years of Upheaval* (Boston: Little, Brown, 1982), pp. 539, 615-616, 624, 749, 789.

[83]Kissinger, *Ibid.*, pp. 627, 637-638, 640, 650.

[84]*Ibid.*, pp. 792, 1078, 1205.

[85]*Ibid.*, pp. 842-843.

[86]"After Lebanon: A Conversation," *The Economist*, Nov. 13-19, 1982, pp. 27-34.

encourage Israel to negotiate. How? It is more likely to do so, he suggests, if it feels compassion or affection rather than unremitting pressure on the part of the U.S. What if this doesn't work? If the U.S. disagrees with Israel on substantive points, he says, it must be prepared to express disagreement—even strongly if necessary. But if pressures must be exerted on Israel, Kissinger argues, the U.S. should be sensitive to its psychic limitations and exert pressure "retail rather than wholesale." As for sanctions, Kissinger can only hope that such a point will never be reached.[87] While it would be impolitic for Kissinger to elaborate upon a hypothetical negotiating process, his marketing terms do little to enlighten us. The question remains: how much influence can the United States exercise over Israel, and how could it or should it be exercised?

Some insight into these questions is provided by former President Carter and his key foreign policy advisors, Secretary of State Cyrus Vance and National Security Advisor Zbigniew Brzezinski. When the Carter Administration took office in 1977, his advisors (contrary to the views of Kissinger) believed that stalemate in the Middle East would gradually fragment, inevitably radicalizing the Arabs and reintroducing the Soviets into the region. Progress toward peace was seen as a means

---

[87] *The Economist*, Nov. 13-19, 1982, p. 30. It should be noted that presidents have threatened sanctions against Israel before. The most frequently cited instance is that by Eisenhower in 1957, when the Israelis were reluctant to withdraw from the Sinai and were threatened by the United States with termination of governmental and private assistance as well as eventual U.N. sanctions and eventual expulsion from the U.N.. Donald Neff, *Warriors at Suez*, pp. 416-417, 430-435. Less well known are other instances such as the warning issued to the Begin government in September 1977 that unless Israel immediately terminated its military operations in Lebanon, the U.S. would halt all military aid to Israel. To Zbigniew Brzezinski, Begin's subsequent order for his troops to withdraw from Lebanon indicated that a firm and clear position by the United States could be sustained, provided that the administration persisted. Zbigniew Brzezinski, *Power and Principle: Memoirs of a National Security Advisor, 1977-1981* (New York: Farrar, Strauss, Giroux, 1983), p. 107.

to achieve both greater security for Israel and a better position for the United States among the moderate Arab states.[88]

President Carter, spurred on by a commitment to human rights and willing to face the necessary political risks to reach a peace settlement, set out in early 1977 to meet with the leaders of the nations involved in the Arab-Israeli conflict and then to put together his concept of what should be done. This accomplished, he intended to put as much pressure as he could on the different parties to accept a solution that was fair. His plan would have to have the full support of the American people, he realized, and would have to be one that could be accepted by Begin in a showdown.[89]

According to Brzezinski and Vance, the plan initially chosen derived from a perception that there were no more "small steps" left to take; hard issues had to be confronted and a comprehensive approach seemed to be the best way. The bedrock of Middle East policy would continue to be a commitment to the security of Israel; along with Israel's right to live in peace and security, however, the president and Vance were convinced that no lasting solution to the Arab-Israeli conflict was possible until "a just answer to the Palestinian question could be found, one almost certainly leading to a Palestinian homeland and some form of self-determination." Carter's preference, according to Vance, was a Palestinian homeland tied to Jordan or a larger confederation. The initial push for a comprehensive peace, however, was overambitious and bore out some of Kissinger's apprehensions about a comprehensive approach. Nevertheless, Brzezinski is probably right when he asserts that without such an effort, it is unlikely that Sadat would have gone to Jerusalem, or that Begin would have made the limited compromises that he did.[90]

Carter's difficulties with former Prime Minister Rabin and then Prime Minister Begin, whom on occasion he apparently saw as a

---

[88]Brzezinski, *Power and Principle*, pp. 83, 277; Vance, *Hard Choices*, pp. 163, 166.

[89]Jimmy Carter, *Keeping Faith*, pp. 277, 284-285, 306, 338.

[90]Brzezinski, *Power and Principle*, pp. 83, 121-122, 154; Vance, *Hard Choices*, pp. 163-164, 177.

"psycho" and not altogether rational,[91] verify Kissinger's descriptions of the conduct of Isræli diplomacy. Carter's aim was to reconcile differences between the Egyptians and Isrælis, between the demands of Isræli security and Palestinian rights—seeking consensus in the belief that reconciliation could, in effect, create a positive-sum game. According to Carter, Sadat seemed to trust him too much, Begin not enough. In Carter's assessment, the Isræli Prime Minister's aims were clear: a separate peace, to keep the West Bank and Gaza, and to avoid the Palestinian issue.[92] In short, as we have seen earlier, Begin regarded the conflict between Isræli security needs and Palestinian rights as a zero-sum game. These differences increased mutual distrust and rendered inevitable their attempts to influence each other by public pressures.

Brzezinski examines in considerable detail the administration's attitudes toward the question of putting pressure on Isræl. Isræli politicians, he believed, could only advocate a genuine compromise if they could argue that U.S.-Isræli relations would suffer; most Isrælis would not defy the U.S. *if* the U.S. meant business. This view, it might be noted, has been expressed by the Isrælis themselves. Former Foreign Minister Abba Eban, when asked whether he was happy with the enormous assistance that the United States has given to Isræl, made the following observation: "In a way, we Isrælis ought to be absolutely grateful. America has given us all the money and weapons and diplomatic support we could ever hope to get. Yet, to be frank, I think you have to risk getting us a bit angry at you. Henry Kissinger and Jimmy Carter made us angry, but, as you remember, they also brought

---

[91]Brzezinski, *Power and Principle*, pp. 262, 264. An incident recorded by Brzezinski reveals, perhaps, some of the behavior that elicited Carter's judgments. After requesting a private meeting with the president preceding the signing of the Egyptian-Isræli treaty, Begin requested that Carter, "as a gesture for Mrs. Begin" (a phrase which he repeated several times), forgive Isræl the outstanding debt on $3 billion in aid it was receiving from the United States. Brzezinski, p.287.

[92]Carter, *Keeping Faith*, pp. 322, 336, 344-345, 409, 422. See also Carter's remarks to the *Christian Science Monitor*, Aug. 15, 1983, where he expresses his belief "that Begin always intended, in effect, to annex the West Bank."

us peace with Egypt.... The new American administration is going to have to push us a bit more to finish this peace process. *That* is the greatest gift you Americans can still give to us—and to all the people in this war-weary area." Brzezinski, who appears to have had similar perceptions, saw Begin's extreme views as an asset in mobilizing on behalf of a genuine settlement a significant portion of the American Jewish community—from whom, Kissinger told him, he could expect a massive onslaught.[93] Vance is more circumspect. Perceived American pressure on Israel, he notes, if it were too heavy, could provoke the Israelis to rally around an uncompromising stance. According to Vance, the hope for peace rested on the capacity of Israeli leaders to resolve their internal divisions, as well as their fears and mistrust of the Arabs. The United States did not want to hobble forces within Israel that were ready to take risks for peace by gratuitous confrontation that appeared to disregard Israel's legitimate security concerns.[94]

Carter, however, was prepared to take a firm stand on the fundamental issues of arms transfers and aid policy, and according to his national security advisor he was prepared to risk losing the presidency for peace. When the possibility of a public showdown was first discussed in the administration, House Speaker Tip O'Neill advised Brzezinski that if the nation were forced to choose between the President and the pro-Israel lobby, and if the choice were clearly put, it would choose the President. Carter never directly presented the country with such a choice, apparently believing that developments did not warrant a debate that would be so divisive. Later, when the stalemated negotiations between Egypt and Israel revived talk of a showdown on the question of settlements between Israel and the United States, Carter asked Senate Majority Leader Robert Byrd if he were willing to have a showdown with Israel in Congress (the answer was yes, although the showdown was avoided).[95]

---

[93]Brzezinski, *Power and Principle*, pp. 88, 96-97. For the Eban quotation, see Jess Gorkin, "Can we Bring Peace to the Middle East?" *Parade Magazine*, Nov. 25, 1984, pp. 19-20.

[94]Vance, *Hard Choices*, pp. 184-185. Vance underscores Israel's internal problems, pp. 237, 242, 254.

[95]Brzezinski, *Power and Principle*, pp. 97, 277-278.

The psychological value of confrontation and public pressure was something that the Carter Administration understood as well as the Begin government. Brzezinski, for one, believed that breakthroughs sometimes required a confrontation. Secretary of State Vance, for another, believed strongly in the need to press Israel on the Palestinian issue. At one point, according to Brzezinski, when the President expressed frustration over Israeli defiance, Vance suggested that the U.S. consider responding to the establishment of further Israeli settlements by removing the self-imposed restraint on not talking with the P.L.O. (the legacy of Sinai II negotiated under Kissinger). On another occasion, according to Brzezinski, Vance suggested initiating contacts with the P.L.O. as a way of generating movement in the peace process. On still another occasion, although the administration had made a conscious decision not to intensify Israeli insecurity by using aid as a source of pressure, he advocated reducing U.S. economic aid to Israel every time the Israelis established a new settlement.[96]

Carter was also adept at using as an element of persuasion his firm grasp of what was acceptable to Israeli public opinion. In negotiating the Camp David accords, the President predicted to Begin that the Israeli people would not agree with their leader that the Sinai settlers were cause for rejecting the peace effort, and that Begin could sell the removal of the settlements to them. On another occasion, he asserted that his position was more representative of Israeli opinion than Begin's. Carter was certain that he and Sadat could come up with an agreement which a majority of Israelis would accept. His major problem was not to convince the Israeli people, but the Israeli Prime Minister, and he was not above using the former to prod the latter. As the President noted in his diary, there was quite a buzz in the Knesset when he told its members that the Israeli people were ready for peace, but that their leaders had not yet shown that they had the courage to take a chance for peace.[97]

The political costs of alienating Israel's many supporters in the U.S., according to Brzezinski, eventually began to be a factor in the administration—affecting first Vice President Mondale (who believed

---

[96]*Ibid.*, pp. 103-106, 108-109, 118, 236, 248, 250, 251, 278, 280, 440-441.

[97]Carter, *Keeping Faith*, pp. 359, 370, 386, 413, 422.

that maximum presidential leverage on Israel extended over the first or second year of office before diminishing because of political costs) and then advisors such as Stuart Eisenstadt and Robert Lipshutz. While Carter continued to seek a comprehensive settlement, changes in tactics were necessitated by Sadat's initiative, by conclusion of the Camp David accords and the Egyptian-Israeli Peace Treaty, and by increasing domestic pressures—all of which contributed to a slackening of the administration's will.[98]

These developments were compounded by Sadat's desire to avoid a showdown on the Palestinian problem until the Sinai was returned. Given other demands on Carter's time, and his preoccupation with Iran, Brzezinski argues that the president would have had to have a reasonable expectation of a genuinely impressive success to justify pressuring Begin (who wanted Carter to be defeated in 1980) and risking a massive public clash with Israel. Failure to obtain Begin's clear-cut agreement on settlement activity suggested that such a success was unlikely.[99] Accordingly, the United States did not assert its position on either the settlements or the autonomy talks, and the peace process went into limbo until it was revived by the Reagan Plan.[100]

---

[98]Brzezinski, *Power and Principle*, pp. 238-239, 254, 279-281, 442-443.

[99]*Ibid.*, pp. 238-239, 273, 279, 443. For differences of interpretation over agreement on settlement activity during the negotiations at Camp David, see fn. 66 earlier in this text.

[100]The Reagan Plan was put forward only after Israel had withdrawn from the Sinai, and it was facilitated by the change in U.S. Secretaries of State. The positive reception the plan received in the United States was undoubtedly due to the Israeli invasion of Lebanon, which created a climate of opinion far more sympathetic to the Arabs than that which existed in 1981 and more conducive to the notion that reasonable U.S. pressures on Israel (reducing or suspending aid to force a pull-out of Israeli forces from Lebanon) was permissible (50 per cent of a national sample and 18 per cent of American Jews agreed, while 38 per cent of a national sample and 75 per cent of American Jews did not). Americans also favored the West Bank's being under Jordanian or Palestinian sovereignty (as opposed to Israeli sovereignty) by a ratio of 54 per cent to 21 per cent (American Jews, on the other hand, favored Israeli sovereignty by a ratio of 58 per cent to 23 per cent). *Newsweek*, Oct. 4, 1982.

Whatever the constraints on U.S. influence over Isræl, American presidents and their closest foreign policy advisors, conscious of the political liabilities, nonetheless have sought repeatedly to exercise whatever influence they can muster in order to induce and prod Isræl to be more responsive to American interests.[101]

President Reagan and Secretary Shultz, in spite of their strong support for Isræl, have not been exceptions. According to one well-informed correspondent, President Reagan promised King Hussein in December 1982 that the United States would try to halt the building of Isræli settlements in the West Bank and Gaza. The president also reportedly told the king that he intended to press the peace plan outlined in his September 1, 1982 initiative even though he knew that by doing so he could lose the Jewish vote in 1984 (as it turned out, Jews voted for Mondale by a ratio of 2:1). Subsequent developments, however, proved the president's resolution to be limited. In March 1984, King Hussein announced that he was not prepared to enter into U.S.-sponsored negotiations with Isræl on the problem of the West Bank. His decision was precipitated by the administration's refusal to support a United Nations draft resolution calling Isræli West Bank settlements illegal, and by the president's rejection of the king's request to use his influence with Isræl to facilitate the attendance of moderate West Bank leaders at the November 1984 meeting of the Palestinian National Council.[102] The American presidential campaign in 1984, meanwhile, showed both major candidates pledging complete support for Isræl and avoiding any specific discussions of the requirements for peace in the region.

---

[101]For threats by the Ford administration (whose policies are otherwise not discussed in this monograph) to suspend American economic and military aid to Isræl, for Kissinger's "reassessment" of American policy, and for the response of the pro-Isræl lobby in the Spring of 1975, see Edward Sheehan, *The Arabs, Isrælis, and Kissinger: A Secret History of American Diplomacy in the Middle East* (New York: Reader's Digest Press, 1976), pp. 159-176.

[102]Karen E. House, *Wall Street Journal*, Apr. 14, 1983; and the interview with King Hussein, *New York Times*, Mar. 15, 1984.

It is doubtful that a second Reagan administration will be any more successful than its predecessors in influencing either the Arab world or Israel to take the steps necessary for peace. Leverage over the former is limited and, other than security assistance, consists primarily of the fact that, more than any other country, the U.S. can (even if it is not always willing to) influence Israeli policies. Leverage over the latter, as we have seen, is not easy to exercise. Current difficulties over the withdrawal of Israeli forces from Lebanon may be resolved, and Israel may eventually accept a list of Palestinian delegates who, along with future compatriots from Jordan, meet with U.S. representatives and later participate in negotiations over the future of the occupied territories. But what will be negotiated? It is here that the question of U.S. influence and determination will be tested. Israel's massive settlement activity on the West Bank and the determination of the Likud coalition to annex the West Bank and Gaza will continue to pose serious obstacles to progress. The national unity government installed in Israel in September 1984, meanwhile, is seriously divided and promises little more than *l'immobilisme* of the Fourth French Republic. In 1986, moreover, Yitzhak Shamir will become prime minister, posing added problems.

In the meantime, speculation over presidential strategy continues—particularly by some who view the Reagan Plan as having had a hidden agenda. The United States would have been naive, they assert, to believe that Begin's mind could ever have been changed. As a consequence, they conceive of the plan as intended not to influence Begin, or his successors, but rather to draw King Hussein into the peace process (i.e., in a manner that exhibits greater commitment than his initiatives to date). The importance of Hussein's involvement, they believe, would be to precipitate within Israel a movement that is responsive to Hussein's initiative and opposed to the policies pursued by the Likud coalition. If a movement were to develop, what would make it significant would be that it could precipitate a coalition crisis, a new election, and a clear Labor majority in the Knesset. Such a development would also legitimize within the United States opposition to the policies of the Likud. U.S. pressure on Israel would be much more effective if it were correctly characterized as anti-Likud rather than anti-Israeli. Common ground between the U.S. government and the Labor Party within Israel would also help destroy the credibility of polemicists in this country who could confuse the ensuing debate by accusing anyone who criticizes policies espoused by the Likud of being anti-Semitic.[103]

A thoughtful analysis by political scientist Ian Lustick argues that American initiatives should be designed to affect Israeli politics rather than Israeli policies, and suggests how it might be possible to create conditions supportive of substantial shifts in Israeli politics. Because his proposals would contribute indirectly to the transformation of values and ideologies underscored by Touval, and could affect the mind sets of the negotiating parties, emphasized by Kissinger, Lustick offers a constructive contribution to a resolution of the Arab-Israeli conflict.[104]

The United States, Lustick asserts, must stop characterizing the present as a not-to-be-missed opportunity; instead, it should prepare for years of patient diplomacy, backed by concrete measures that shape the context of Israeli policies. He opposes direct use of Israel's military and economic dependence on the United States to manipulate Israeli policies or politics. Such a course, he argues, would generate a severe backlash in Israel, raise a storm of protest in the United States, and send a dangerous signal to the Arabs that concessions from them are unnecessary. Lustick would prefer to use leverage in a less confrontational, more indirect manner. One of the measures he suggests is voicing opinion about the legal status of the settlements. According to the 1907 Hague Convention and a unanimous declaration by Israel's High Court of Justice, he points out, any "permanent" settlement is *ipso facto* illegal.[105]

According to former Secretary of State Vance, the long-standing U.S. position on settlements is that they are contrary to international

---

[103] See, for example, Norman Podhoretz, "J'Accuse," *Commentary* 74 (Sept. 1982), pp. 21-31, and the discussion in the Dec. 1982 issue. For a discussion of Reagan and the Jewish vote, see Arthur Hertzberg, "Reagan and the Jews," *New York Review of Books*, Jan. 31, 1985, pp. 11-14.

[104] Ian S. Lustick, "Israeli Politics and American Foreign Policy," *Foreign Affairs* 61 (Winter 1982/83), pp. 379-399.

[105] Lustick, "Israeli Politics and American Foreign Policy," pp. 392-398.

law and an obstacle to peace. President Reagan's position, however, has been more difficult to define. It includes a statement in February 1981 that the settlements might have been ill-advised and unnecessarily provocative, but not illegal; a statement in May 1983 that Israeli settlements did not pose an "obstacle" to peace; and a veto in August 1983 of a U.N. Security Council resolution that said Israeli settlements in the West Bank had no legal validity and were a major and serious obstruction to peace. The administration's objection to the resolution rested in part on the judgment that characterization of Israeli settlement policy as having no legal standing is inconsistent with the views of the United States. A State Department spokesman also asserted that the resolution's call for dismantlement of existing settlements was impractical and that the implication that Israel was expelling the Arab population from the occupied territories was unfounded. King Hussein refused to accept the U.S. explanation of its veto, which he regarded as "totally unacceptable, inadequate and unsatisfactory." Unless the United States can clarify its position and speak with one voice about the settlements, voicing opinion about their legality (or illegality) will have little effect on Israel. Israeli settlement activity, according to American and Egyptian officials, more than anything else undermined the credibility of the Camp David process. Until it ceases, it is hard to see how the United States can have any credibility as a mediator in the Arab world.[106]

Lustick also advocates giving concrete effect to U.S. opposition to Israeli settlements. He supports deducting from aid to Israel amounts estimated to have been spent in the previous year on settlements in the occupied territories. "The key to success," Lustick observes, "lies in the convincing promotion of U.S. ideas that affect the rhetorical and political resources available to competing Israeli groups." While former Defense Minister Moshe Arens has said that Israeli expenditures on the West Bank "are the last investments we would give up under the most stringent conditions because we feel that our very physical security depends on what we do in Judea and Samaria," Lustick's suggestion,

[106]Vance, *Hard Choices*, pp. 185, 231, 237, 354; Evans and Novak, *Washington Post*, June 20, 1983; Ian Black, *Washington Post*, Aug. 4 1982; *Washington Post*, Aug. 21, 1983; *International Herald Tribune*, Aug. 4, 1983; *New York Times*, Mar. 15, 1984.

particularly if it were carried out on a progressive basis, could have considerably more influence than Arens is willing to acknowledge. Israel is not spending *millions* of dollars on West Bank settlements; it is spending *billions*.[107]

Finding the right combination of carrot and stick that would cause Israel to take the steps necessary for peace requires more imagination and will than recent administrations have devoted to the task.[108]

---

[107]Lustick, "Israeli Politics and American Foreign Policy," pp. 390, 393-94; for Arens' statement, see Sally Weymouth, *Washington Post*, July 24, 1983. On November 29, 1982, the Israeli press carried estimates by Michael Dekel, Deputy Minister of Agriculture, that the cost of every Jewish family settled in the West Bank ran from 4 to 5 million shekels. Current exchange rates would have made that $90,000 per family, or $630 million for 7,000 families; housing was to be available before October 1983. Required government financing for the third Drobles Plan, named after the head of the settlement department of the World Zionist Organization and tacitly if not formally approved by the Israeli government, which calls for the establishment of 57 more settlements by 1987, runs to 12 billion Israeli shekels, or $240 million annually. Another report suggests that costs may be as high as $1.5 billion over the next three years. Trudy Rubin, *Christian Science Monitor*, Aug. 17, 26, 1983. Harry J. Shaw, Senior Associate of the Carnegie Endowment for International Peace, estimates the annual cost of Israel's West Bank settlements at $400 million *Christian Science Monitor*, Dec.19, 1984. Government subsidies include infrastructure, roads, electricity, water, communications, and low-interest long-term mortgages that are not indexed to Israeli inflation and offer a variety of rebates (e.g., for military service, having been wounded, being a refugee, having children). The majority of settlers, particularly in the urban settlements that serve as dormitory suburbs for Jerusalem and Tel-Aviv, are not motivated by ideology. They are mostly young, middle class, Ashkenazim responding to the fact that subsidized housing on the West Bank is 50 per cent to 60 per cent of the cost of housing in Israel. These observations are based on conversations with Palestinians and Israelis and travel in the West Bank and Israel in April 1983.

[108]Israeli leaders have repeatedly rejected U.S. guarantees of a comprehensive settlement as being meaningless. In March 1977, Prime Minister Yitzhak Rabin told President Carter that

Clearly, the United States can provide a considerable number of incentives—beyond massive economic aid—for Israel to cooperate with well-conceived initiatives. Security arrangements and U.S. guarantees, for example, could help to compensate for the loss of strategic depth on the West Bank; such guarantees could be made more credible by an Israeli stake in the western alliance and could establish the important principle of interdependence between the U.S. and Israel.

But providing Israel with guarantees, aid, and support, *without* a constructive Israeli response to American interests in general, and to White House peace initiatives in particular, is counterproductive because it deprives the United States of important leverage in the negotiations that must take place. [109] Such a course of action reduces

---

the only commitment Israel wanted from the United States was to supply arms. Vance, *Hard Choices*, p.173. Such a commitment, of course, would give the Israelis license to do what they want without consideration for U.S. interests. As President Nixon told leaders of the American Jewish community in June 1974, hardware alone was a policy that no longer made sense. Each new war would be more costly, there were more Arabs than Israelis, and whether Israel could survive over a long period of time against these odds was questionable. In addition, the United States would inevitably be drawn in, as it was in 1973. Nixon's recommendation was that Israel seek a settlement now, while it was in a position of strength. His message was clear: Israel could not have a blank check when it came to American arms. Nixon, *RN, the Memoirs of Richard Nixon*, p. 1007.

[109]In June 1983, Secretary of Defense Weinberger noted that the military cooperation agreement, signed on November 30, 1981, and suspended on December 18, 1981, over the extension of Israeli civil law to the Golan, might soon be revived. Hedrick Smith, *International Herald Tribune*, June 16, 1983. The *quid pro quo* presumably had to do not with settlements, but with Israeli willingness to withdraw from Lebanon. This interpretation was borne out in November when, according to Prime Minister Shamir, the U.S. and Israel established a joint military-political committee to coordinate enhanced co-operation. The U.S. also agreed to increase military grant aid to Israel and to negotiate a free-trade agreement with Israel. *Washington Post*, Nov. 30, 1983. The question that should be

one of Israel's primary incentives to freeze its settlement activities; it also eliminates one of the factors most likely to bring home to the Israelis the enormous cost of continuing their unenlightened policies toward the West Bank and Gaza.

The United States can wield a stick, force the Israelis to respond to U.S. interests, and coerce them into supporting U.S. peace initiatives only at the risk of feeding their worst fears and causing them to become absolutely intransigent. Clearly, the impetus toward autonomy for the Palestinians, and hence toward a settlement of the Palestinian problem, must come from the Israelis themselves; it must come from internal debates and careful assessments of their current policies. This development is possible, however, only if the United States allows it to evolve naturally and does not impede it by making it possible for the Israelis to avoid the consequences—economic, political, and moral—of the policies they choose to pursue. The argument here is that the United States should provide the carrot, but in such a way as to allow the Israeli government to confront the fact that it wields its own stick.

---

posed is whether or not the United States should back away from greater military cooperation with Israel and avoid further relief of Israel's financial burdens until there is a *quid pro quo* on the problem of settlement activity.

PART TWO

BIBLIOGRAPHICAL ESSAY

by

Michael Rubner

REFERENCES

The literature on the Arab-Israeli conflict is voluminous, and it has grown at an exponential rate in recent years. Consequently, the following bibliography is necessarily selective in a number of ways.

First, it includes only those references that illuminate the issues raised in the preceding monograph. Second, as a research tool for both generalists and specialists, it contains primarily books, articles and monographs that meet the essential requirements of scholarly investigation; with a few notable exceptions, works of a highly polemical nature have been deliberately excluded. Third, it includes only those items that are currently available in English and that are likely to be accessible to American readers. Fourth, in order to minimize duplication of other bibliographies, a deliberate attempt was made to include the most pertinent publications that have appeared during the past decade. Finally, special care was exercised to ensure presentation of a variety of diverse perspectives on what has become one of the most complex and emotionally volatile conflicts in the 20th century.

To enhance the utility of the bibliography, entries have been classified under twenty-eight separate headings. While space limitations precluded annotation of all individual entries, the most significant items are identified and briefly highlighted under each heading. Because any single item often focuses on a number of issues, readers are urged to consult relevant entries that might have been classified under related categories.

Those wishing to keep abreast of rapidly changing developments in the Middle East may want to consult regularly two outstanding reference sources. Each issue of the *Middle East Journal*, a quarterly published by the Middle East Institute, contains an extensive bibliography of recent books and periodical literature on the Arab-Israeli conflict. Likewise, every edition of the *Journal of Palestine Studies*, a quarterly published by the Institute for Palestine Studies, includes a chronology, translated excerpts of articles from the Arab, Israeli, and international press, as well as documentary source materials and a bibliography of periodical literature on the Arab-Israeli conflict.

Bibliographies

The compilation by DeVore (entry 1) contains 3,000 entries on the Arab-Jewish conflict in Palestine from the beginning of the 20th century to the October 1973 war. The annotated bibliography by Khalidi and Khadduri (entry 3) focuses on the emergence of Palestine as a political issue and includes entries in English, Arabic, Hebrew, French, German and Russian. Sherman (entry 5) has compiled a list of 3,700 items of selected writings in English on the Arab-Israeli conflict.

1   DeVore, Ronald M. *The Arab-Israeli Conflict: A Historical, Political, Social and Military Bibliography* . Santa Barbara, CA: Clio, 1976.

2   Hussaini, Hatem I., ed. *The Palestine Problem: An Annotated Bibliography, 1967-1980*. Washington, D.C.: Palestine Information Office, 1980.

3   Khalidi, Walid, and Jill Khadduri, eds. *Palestine and the Arab-Israeli Conflict*. Beirut: Institute for Palestine Studies, 1975.

4   Rubner, Michael. *Conflict in the Middle East from October 1973 to July 1976: A Selected Bibliography*. Political Issues Series, Vol. 4, No. 4. Los Angeles: Center for the Study of Armament and Disarmament, California State University, 1977.

5   Sherman, John, ed. *The Arab-Israeli Conflict, 1945-1971: A Bibliography.* New York: Garland, 1978.

The Arab-Israeli Conflict:

General Works

This section contains several books that are especially useful to those seeking background material on the historical evolution of the Middle East conflict. Excellent historical surveys of the roots of the impasse between Zionism and Palestinian nationalism can be found in the works by Flapan (entry 9), Hirst (entry 14), Kayyali (entry 16), Khouri (entry 17), Ovendale (entry 23), and Regan (entry 26). Edward Said analyzes the ideological foundations of Zionism and describes the development of Palestinian national consciousness from a pro-

Palestinian perspective (entry 29), whereas Halkin (entry 12) supplies a pro-Zionist critique of Said.

The volumes by Laqueur and Rubin (entry 18), Lukacs (entry 19), Moore (entry 21) and Rabinovich and Reinharz (entry 25) contain important documents on various aspects of the Jewish-Arab conflict, while Dupuy (entry 8) and Herzog (entry 13) analyze the military histories of the Arab-Israeli wars since 1948.

Cattan (entry 7) and the Mallisons (entry 20) treat legal issues in the Arab-Israeli conflict in a manner sympathetic to the Arab-Palestinian side, while Stone focuses on the same issues from a pro-Israeli perspective (entry 30). The role of the United Nations in the Palestine controversy is ably examined by Nuseibeh (entry 22) and Pogany (entry 24).

Although it contains few original insights, the book by former President Jimmy Carter (entry 6) is rich in details and covers events up to the end of 1984.

6   Carter, Jimmy. *The Blood of Abraham: Insights into the Middle East*. Boston: Houghton Mifflin, 1985.

7   Cattan, Henry. *Palestine and International Law: The Legal Aspects of the Arab-Israeli Conflict*. 2d ed. New York: Longman, 1976.

8   Dupuy, Trevor N. *Elusive Victory: The Arab-Israeli Wars, 1947-1974*. New York: Harper & Row, 1978.

9   Flapan, Simha. *Zionism and the Palestinians*. New York: Barnes & Noble, 1979.

10   Fraser, T. G. *The Middle East, 1914-1979*. New York: St. Martin's, 1980.

11   Freedman, Robert O., ed. *World Politics and the Arab-Israeli Conflict*. Elmsford, NY.: Pergamon, 1979.

12   Halkin, Hillel. "Whose Palestine? An Open Letter to Edward Said." *Commentary* 69 (May 1980), 21-30.

13   Herzog, Chaim. *The Arab-Israeli Wars*. New York: Random House, 1982.

14   Hirst, David. *The Gun and the Olive Branch: The Roots of Violence in the Middle East*. 2d ed. London & Boston: Faber & Faber, 1984.

15   Hudson, Michael, ed. *Alternative Approaches to the Arab-Israeli Conflict: A Comparative Analysis of the Principal Actors*. London: Croom Helm, 1983.

16   Kayyali, A. W. *Palestine: A Modern History*. London: Third World Center for Research & Publishing, 1981.

17   Khouri, Fred J. *The Arab-Israeli Dilemma*. 2d. ed. Syracuse: Syracuse University Press, 1976.

18   Laqueur, Walter, and Barry Rubin, eds. *The Israel-Arab Reader: A Documentary History of the Middle East Conflict*. New York: Penguin, 1984.

19   Lukacs, Yehuda., ed. *Documents on the Israeli-Palestinian Conflict, 1967-1983*. New York: Cambridge University Press, 1984.

20   Mallison, Sally V., and W. Thomas Mallison. *The Palestinian Problem in International Law and World Order*. New York: Longman, 1983.

21   Moore, John Norton, ed. *The Arab-Israeli Conflict: Readings and Documents*. Princeton: Princeton University Press, 1977.

22   Nuseibeh, Hazem Zaki. *Palestine and the United Nations*. New York: Quartet Books, 1982.

23   Ovendale, Ritchie. *The Origins of the Arab-Israeli Wars*. New York: Longman, 1984.

24   Pogany, Istvan S. *The Security Council and the Arab-Israeli Conflict*. New York: St. Martin's, 1984.

25   Rabinovich, Itamar, and Jehuda Reinharz, eds. *Israel in the Middle East: Documents and Readings on Society, Politics and Foreign Relations, 1948-Present*. New York: Oxford University Press, 1984.

26   Regan, Geoffrey B. *Israel and the Arabs*. New York: Cambridge University Press, 1984.

27   Richardson, John P. *The West Bank: A Portrait*. Washington, D.C.: Middle East Institute, 1984.

28   Rubinstein, Alvin Z., ed. *The Arab-Israeli Conflict: Perspectives*. New York: Praeger, 1984.

29   Said, Edward. *The Question of Palestine*. New York: Times Book, 1979.

30   Stone, Julius. *Israel and Palestine: Assault on the Law of Nations*. Baltimore: Johns Hopkins University Press, 1981.

31   Touval, Saadia. *The Peace Brokers: Mediators in the Arab-Israeli Conflict, 1948-1979*. Princeton: Princeton University Press, 1982.

Palestinians:

General Accounts

The books by Dimbleby (entry 35), Epp and Goddard (entry 36), Gilmour (entry 39), Smith (entry 45), and Stewart (entry 47) contain sympathetic accounts of the plight of the Palestinians both before and after the creation of Israel in 1948. Issues pertaining to the problem of Palestinian homelessness are taken up by Nazzal (entry 43) and Radley (entry 44), and the implications of the presence of numerous Palestinian exiles in Lebanon are examined by Faris (entry 37) and Farsoun and Wingerter (entry 38).

The anthologies edited by Ben-Dor (entry 32), Curtis (entry 34), and Migdal (entry 41) include many essays by Israeli and non-Palestinian scholars on Palestinian political and social history, relations between the Palestinians and the Arab states, and contemporary social and political aspects of the Palestinian community.

Written by American and Israeli scholars, the articles in the volume edited by Gruen (entry 40) attempt to cast a different light on the issue by arguing that the Palestinian problem is neither the central nor the only dilemma for American policy in the Middle East.

32   Ben-Dor, Gabriel, ed. *The Palestinians and the Middle East Conflict*. Ramat Gan, Israel: Turtledove, 1978.

33   Cooley, John K. *Green March, Black September: The Story of the Palestinian Arabs*. London: Frank Cass, 1973.

34   Curtis, Michael, et al., eds. *The Palestinians: People, History, Politics*. New Brunswick, NJ: Transaction Books, 1975.

35   Dimbleby, Jonathan. *The Palestinians*. New York: Quartet Books, 1984.

36   Epp, Frank, and John Goddard. *The Palestinians: Portrait of a People in Conflict*. Scottdale, PA.: Herald Press, 1976.

37   Faris, H. "Lebanon and the Palestinians: Brotherhood or Fratricide?" *Arab Studies Quarterly* 3:4 (1981), 352-370.

38   Farsoun, S., and R. Wingerter. "The Palestinians in Lebanon." *SAIS Review* No. 3 (1981-82), 93-106.

39   Gilmour, David. *Dispossessed: The Ordeal of the Palestinians*. London: Sphere Books, 1982.

40   Gruen, George E., ed. *The Palestinians in Perspective: Implications for Mideast Peace and U.S. Policy*. New York: Institute of Human Relations Press, the American Jewish Committee, 1982.

41   Migdal, Joel, ed. *Palestinian Society and Politics*. Princeton, NJ.: Princeton University Press. 1980.

42   Nakhleh, Khalil, and Elia Zureik, eds. *The Sociology of the Palestinians*. London: Croom Helm, 1980.

43   Nazzal, Nafez. *The Palestinian Exodus from Galilee, 1948*. Beirut: Institute for Palestine Studies, 1978.

44   Radley, Kurt R. "The Palestinian Refugees: The Right to Return in International Law." *American Journal of International Law* 72 (July 1978), 586-614.

45   Smith, Pamela Ann. *Palestine and the Palestinians, 1876-1983*. New York: St. Martin's, 1984.

46   Sobel, Lester, ed. *Palestinian Impasse: Arab Guerrillas and International Terror.* New York: Facts on File, 1977.

47   Stewart, Desmond. *Palestinians: Victims of Expediency.* London: Quartet Books, 1982.

48   Tahir, Jamil M. "An Assessment of Palestinian Human Resources: Higher Education and Manpower." *Journal of Palestine Studies* 14 (Spring 1985), 32-53.

49   Zureik, Elia T. "The Palestinians in the Consciousness of Israeli Youth." *Journal of Palestine Studies* 4 (Winter 1975), 52-75.

50.   _____. "Toward a Sociology of the Palestinians." *Journal of Palestine Studies* 6 (Summer 1977), 3-16.

Palestinian Nationalism

The emergence of a distinctive Palestinian nationalism during the British Mandatory period and its resurgence since the mid-1960s tended to exacerbate the political conflicts between Jews and Arabs and later between Israel and the Palestinians. The standard works on the evolution of Palestinian nationalism are those by Lesch (entry 58), Porath (entries 62 and 63), and Quandt, et al. (entry 64). The volumes by Abu-Lughod (entry 52), Jureidini and Hazen (entry 56), O'Neill (entry 61), and Sayigh (entry 66) focus on the nexus between the suppression of Palestinian aspirations to national self-determination and the rise of organized armed resistance against Zionism and Israel.

The central theme of Ma'oz (entry 59), Mishal (entry 60), Weaver (entry 70), and the articles in the volume edited by Scholch (entry 68) is that the 1967 war and the subsequent Israeli occupation of the West Bank strengthened the Palestinian identity. Sayigh (entry 67) and the Kurodas (entry 57) explain the political socialization processes through which feelings of national consciousness have been transmitted and inculcated among Palestinians in Lebanon and Jordan, respectively.

51   Abu Iyad. *My Home, My Land: A Narrative of the Palestine Struggle.* Translated by Linda Butler. New York: Quadrangle/ New York Times Book, 1981.

52   Abu-Lughod, Ibrahim, ed. *Palestinian Rights: Affirmation and Denial.* Wilmette, IL: Medina Press, 1982.

53   Austin, G. "Palestinian Nationalism: Is it Viable?" *SAIS Review* 4:1 (1984), 161-178.

54   Graham-Brown, Sarah. *Education, Repression, Liberation: Palestinians*. London: World University Press, 1984.

55   Johnson, Nels. *Islam and the Politics of Meaning in Palestinian Nationalism*. London: Kegan Paul, 1982.

56   Jureidini, Paul, and William E. Hazen. *The Palestinian Movement in Politics*. Lexington, MA: Lexington, 1976.

57   Kuroda, Alice K., and Yasumasa Kuroda. *Palestinians Without Palestine: A Study of Political Socialization Among Palestinian Youths*. Washington, D.C.: University Press of America, 1978.

58   Lesch, Ann M. *Arab Politics in Palestine, 1917-1939: The Frustration of a National Movement*. Ithaca, NY: Cornell University Press, 1979.

59   Ma'oz, Moshe. *Palestinian Nationalism: The West Bank Dimension*. Washington, D.C.: Wilson Center, International Security Studies Program, Working Paper 18, 1980.

60   Mishal, Shaul. "Nationalism Through Localism: Some Observations on the West Bank Political Elite." *Middle East Studies* 17:4 (1981), 477-491.

61   O'Neill, Bard E. *Armed Struggle in Palestine: An Analysis of the Palestinian Guerrilla Movement*. Boulder, CO: Westview, 1979.

62   Porath, Yehoshua. *The Emergence of the Palestinian-Arab National Movement, 1918-1929*. Vol. 1. London: Frank Cass, 1974.

63. _____. *The Palestinian Arab National Movement: From Riots to Rebellion, 1929-1939*. Vol. 2. London: Frank Cass, 1977.

64   Quandt, William B., Fuad Jabber, and Ann Mosely Lesch. *The Politics of Palestinian Nationalism*. Los Angeles: University of California Press, 1973.

65   Ramati, Yohanan. "Palestinian Nationalism." *Midstream* 26 (December 1980), 7-10.

66   Sayigh, Rosemary.   *Palestinians: From Peasants to Revolutionaries*. New York: Monthly Review Press, 1979.

67. _____. "Sources of Palestinian Nationalism: A Study of a Palestinian Camp in Lebanon." *Journal of Palestine Studies* 6 (Summer 1977), 17-40.

68   Scholch, Alexander, ed.   *Palestinians over the Green Line: Studies on the Relations Between Palestinians on both Sides of the Armistice Line Since 1967*. London: Ithaca Press, 1983.

69   Tillman, Seth. "Israel and Palestinian Nationalism." *Journal of Palestine Studies* 9 (Autumn 1979), 46-66.

70   Weaver, Thomas P., et al. "What Palestinians Believe: A Systematic Analysis of Belief Systems in the West Bank and Gaza." *Journal of Palestine Studies* 14 (Spring 1985), 110-126.

The Palestine Liberation Organization

Although it was created in 1964, the P.L.O. did not emerge as an important autonomous actor until 1967. In October 1974, an agreement by twenty Arab heads of state recognized the P.L.O. as "the sole legitimate representative of the Palestinian people on any liberated Palestinian territory," and by 1977 more than 100 states had granted the P.L.O. some form of recognition.

The political philosophy guiding the P.L.O. is embodied in the 1968 Palestine National Covenant which asserted that "the partition of Palestine in 1947 and the establishment of the state of Israel are illegal," and that "armed struggle is the only way to liberate Palestine." The origins and implications of several successive versions of the Palestinian Covenant are analyzed in detail from a critical Israeli perspective by Harkabi (entry 84).

The most comprehensive and enlightening accounts of the history, organizational structure, and internal struggles of the P.L.O. from its inception until the eventual evacuation of its leadership from Beirut in 1982 can be found in Becker (entry 74), Cobban (entry 75), and Rubenberg (entry 88). The works by Amos (entry 73), Dobson (entry 76), El-Rayyes and Nahas (entry 77) and Sharabi (entry 90) describe and assess the guerrilla activities of the various constituent commando groups of the P.L.O.

Gresh (entry 82), Miller (entry 86), Muslih (entry 87) and Stanley (entry 92) focus on the causes and consequences of internal rivalries and ideological fragmentation within the P.L.O. The works by Alexander (entry 71). Farsoun (entry 78), Golan (entry 80), Schapiro (entry 89) and Taylor (entry 94) discuss the relationships between the P.L.O., the Arab states, and the superpowers.

71 Alexander, Yonah. "Some Soviet-PLO Linkages." *Middle East Review* 14 (Spring-Summer 1982), 64-70.

72 _____. "The Nature of the PLO: Some International Implications." *Middle East Review* 12:3 (1980), 42-51.

73 Amos, John W., II. *Palestinian Resistance: Organization of a Nationalist Movement.* Elmsford, NY: Pergamon, 1980.

74 Becker, Jillian. *The PLO: The Rise and Fall of the Palestine Liberation Organization.* New York: St. Martin's, 1984.

75 Cobban, Helena. *The Palestinian Liberation Organization: People, Power and Politics.* New York: Cambridge University Press, 1984.

76 Dobson, Christopher. *Black September: Its Short, Violent History.* New York: Macmillan, 1974.

77 El-Rayyes, Riad, and Dunia Nahas. *Guerrillas for Palestine.* London: Croom Helm, 1976.

78 Farsoun, Samih K. "The Palestinians, the PLO and U.S. Foreign Policy." *American-Arab Affairs*, No. 1 (Summer 1982), 81-94.

79 Frangi, Abdallah. *The PLO and Palestine.* Translated by Paul Knight. Totowa, NJ: Zed Press, 1983.

80 Golan, Galia. *The Soviet Union and the Palestine Liberation Organization: An Uneasy Alliance.* New York: Praeger, 1980.

81 Goldberg, J. "The PLO's Position in the Arab-Israeli Conflict in the 1970's." *Orient* 23 (January 1982), 81-92.

82 Gresh, Alain. *The PLO: The Struggle Within; Toward an Independent Palestinian State.* London: Zed Books, 1984.

83   Hamid, Rashid. "What is the PLO?" *Journal of Palestine Studies* 4 (Summer 1975), 90-109.

84   Harkabi, Yehoshafat. *The Palestinian Covenant and Its Meaning*. Totowa, NJ: Valentine, Mitchell, 1979.

85   Lewis, Bernard. "The Palestinians and the PLO: A Historical Approach." *Commentary* 59 (January 1975), 32-48.

86   Miller, Aaron David. *The PLO and the Politics of Survival*. New York: Praeger , with the Center for Strategic and International Studies, Georgetown University, 1983.

87   Muslih, Muhammad Y. "Moderates and Rejectionists Within the Palestine Liberation Organization." *Middle East Journal* 30 (Spring 1976), 127-140.

88   Rubenberg, Cheryl. *The Palestinian Liberation Organization: Its Institutional Infrastructure*. Belmont, MA: Institute of Arab Studies, 1983.

89   Schapiro, L. "The Soviet Union and the PLO." *Survey* 23:3 (1977-78), 193-207.

90   Sharabi, Hisham. *Palestine Guerrillas: Their Credibility and Effectiveness*. Beirut: Institute for Palestine Studies, 1970.

91   Shemesh, M. "The Founding of the PLO, 1964." *Middle East Studies* 20 (October 1984), 105-141.

92   Stanley, Bruce. "Fragmentation and National Liberation Movements: The PLO." *Orbis* 22 (Winter 1979), 1033-1055.

93   Steinberg, Matti. "The PLO and the Mini-Settlement." *Jerusalem Quarterly*, No. 21 (Fall 1981), 129-144.

94   Taylor, Alan R. "The PLO in Inter-Arab Politics." *Journal of Palestine Studies* 11 (Winter 1982), 70-81.

95   Wolffsohn, M. "Israel's PLO Policy, 1977-1981: Towards a Dialogue?" *Orient* 22 (September 1981), 413-430.

96 Yodfat, Aryeh Y., and Yuval Arnon-Ohanna. *PLO Strategy and Tactics*. New York: St. Martin's, 1981.

Israeli Occupation of the West Bank:

General Works

Following the 1967 War, Israel occupied the West Bank, Gaza Strip, Sinai Peninsula, and Golan Heights. While it eventually withdrew from the Sinai in 1982, Israel has refused to relinquish the West Bank and Gaza Strip and continues to exercise control over approximately 1.2 million Palestinian Arabs residing in these areas.

Two diametrically opposed views on the legality of Israel's occupation are presented by Jordan's Crown Prince Hassan (entry 100) who challenges Israeli claims, and by Gerson (entry 106), who defends Israel's rights as a belligerent occupier.

The works by Aruri (entry 99), Gack and Wobcke (entry 104), Metzger, et al. (entry 112) and Nisan (entry 114) are useful references about the general mechanics of Israeli occupation policies in the West Bank, while Stauffer (entry 116), Stork (entry 117), Van Arkadie (entry 119) and Zureik (entry 120) focus on the economic benefits that Israel has derived from its control of the area West of the Jordan River. The intent of former Prime Minister Begin's Likud government to claim Judea and Samaria as part of a Greater Israel is examined by Feldman (entry 103) and Heller (entry 108).

97 Abu-Ayyash, Abdul-Ilah. "Israeli Regional Planning Policy in the Occupied Territories." *Journal of Palestine Studies* 5 (Spring-Summer 1976), 83-108.

98 Aronson, Geoffrey. "Israel's Policy of Military Occupation." *Journal of Palestine Studies* 7 (Summer 1978), 79-98.

99 Aruri, Naseer H., ed. *Occupation: Israel over Palestine*. Belmont, MA: Association of Arab-American University Graduates Press, 1983.

100 Bin Talal, Crown Prince Hassan. *Palestinian Self-Determination: A Study of the West Bank and Gaza Strip*. New York: Quartet Books, 1981.

101   Elazar, Daniel J., ed. *Governing Peoples and Territories.* Philadelphia: Institute for the Study of Human Issues, 1982.

102   _____. *Judea, Samaria and Gaza: Views on the Present and Future.* Washington, D.C.: American Enterprise Institute, 1982.

103   Feldman, Egal. "Conflict or Consensus in Israeli Visions of Judea and Samaria?" *Middle East Review* 15 (Spring-Summer 1983), 45-52.

104   Gack, Christopher, and Manfred Wobcke. *Israel and the Occupied Territories.* New York: Hippocrene, 1981.

105   George, Donald E. *Israeli Occupation: International Law and Political Realities.* Hicksville, NY: Exposition Press, 1980.

106   Gerson, Allan. *Israel, the West Bank and International Law.* Totowa, NJ: Frank Cass, 1978.

107   Hallaj, Muhammad. "Israel's West Bank Gamble." *American-Arab Affairs*, No. 9 (Summer 1984), 95-105.

108   Heller, Mark. "Begin's False Autonomy." *Foreign Policy*, No. 37 (Winter 1979/80), 111-132.

109   Hertzberg, Arthur. "Israel and the West Bank: The Implications of Permanent Control." *Foreign Affairs* 61 (Summer 1983), 1064-1077.

110   Jiryis, Sabri. "Israeli Rejectionism." *Journal of Palestine Studies* 8 (Autumn 1978), 61-84.

111   Litany, Y. "Tragedy on the West Bank." *Dissent* 20, No. 4 (1983), 426-433.

112   Metzger, Jan, et al. *This Land is Our Land: The West Bank Under Israeli Occupation.* London: Zed Press, 1983.

113   Nakhleh, Emile A. "The West Bank and Gaza: People, Perceptions, and Policies." *American-Arab Affairs*, No. 1 (Summer 1982), 95-103.

114   Nisan, Mordechai. *Israel and the Territories: A Case Study in Control: 1967-1977.* Ramat Gan, Israel: Turtledove, 1978.

115 Oren, Michael. "A Horseshoe in the Glove: Milson's Year on the West Bank." *Middle East Review* 16 (Fall 1983), 17-29.

116 Stauffer, Thomas R. "The Price of Peace: The Spoils of War." *American-Arab Affairs*, No. 1 (Summer 1982), 43-54.

117 Stork, Joe. "Water and Israel's Occupation Strategy." *MERIP Reports* 13 (July-August 1983), 19-24.

118 U.S. Congress. House. Committee on Foreign Affairs. *The Situation on the West Bank. Hearing before the Subcommittee on Europe and the Middle East. May 26, 1982.* Washington, D.C.: 1983.

119 Van Arkadie, Brian. *Benefits and Burdens: A Report on the West Bank and Gaza Strip Economies Since 1967.* New York and Washington, D.C.: Carnegie Endowment for International Peace, 1977.

120 Zureik, Elia T. "The Economics of Dispossession: The Palestinians." *Third World Quarterly* 5 (1983), 775-900.

Palestinians under Israeli Occupation

The works in this section provide ample evidence that Israel's occupation has had severe political and psychological impact on the inhabitants of the West Bank. Ma'oz (entry 125) and Tamari (entry 130) document the failure of Israeli efforts to nurture a native West Bank political leadership, whether Palestinian-nationalist or one oriented toward Jordan. Lesch (entry 124) argues that Israel's occupation has generated strong consensus among the Palestinians for an independent state alongside Israel.

Raja Shehadeh, a Palestinian lawyer (entry 128), and Raymonda Tawil, a Palestinian activist who had been arrested by Israeli authorities for alleged contacts with the PLO (entry 132), provide vivid personal accounts of the harshness of Israeli rule. *Arabs Under Israeli Occupation,* 1981 (entry 122) is the tenth volume in an annual series documenting Israeli violations of human rights in the occupied areas.

121 Antonius, Soraya. "Fighting on Two Fronts: Conversations with Palestinian Women." *Journal of Palestine Studies* 8 (Spring 1979), 26-45.

122 *Arabs Under Israeli Occupation, 1981.* Beirut: Institute for Palestine Studies, 1984.

123 Baransi, Salih. "Oral History: The Story of a Palestinian Under Occupation." *Journal of Palestine Studies* 11 (Autumn 1981), 3-30.

124 Lesch, Ann Mosely. *Political Perceptions of the Palestinians on the West Bank and the Gaza Strip.* Washington, D.C.: Middle East Institute, 1980.

125 Ma'oz, Moshe, with Mordechai Nisan. *Palestinian Leadership on the West Bank: The Changing Role of the Mayors Under Jordan and Israel.* London: Frank Cass, 1984.

126 Rockwell, Susan. "Palestinian Women Workers in the Israeli-Occupied Gaza Strip." *Journal of Palestine Studies* 14 (Winter 1985), 114-136.

127 Sayigh, Rosemary. "Encounters with Palestinian Women Under Occupation." *Journal of Palestine Studies* 10 (Summer 1981), 3-26.

128 Shehadeh, Raja. *Samed: Journal of a West Bank Palestinian.* New York: Adama Books, 1984.

129 Shemesh, M. "The West Bank: Rise and Decline of Traditional Leadership, June 1967 to October 1973." *Middle East Studies* 20 (July 1984), 290-323.

130 Tamari, Salim. "In League with Zion: Israel's Search for a Native Pillar." *Journal of Palestine Studies* 12 (Summer 1983), 41-56.

131 Tanber, George J. *Life Under Israeli Occupation.* Washington, D.C.: National Association of Arab Americans, 1981.

132 Tawil, Raymonda Hawa. *My Home, My Prison.* Totowa, NJ: Zed Press, 1983.

133 *The Bitter Year: Arabs Under Israeli Occupation in 1982.* Washington, D.C.: The American-Arab Anti-Discrimination Committee, 1983.

Israeli Occupation and Human Rights Issues

The common theme underlying the selections below is that Israeli authorities have systematically violated various fundamental human rights of Palestinians in the West Bank and Gaza. The prevalence of repressive policies, including arbitrary arrests, lengthy detention without trial, confiscation of property, torture, and deportation is brought to light in the articles by Aruri (entry 136), Bishara (entry 137), Goldstein (entry 141), Jiryis (entry 143) and Lesch (entries 145 and 146).

While severe accusations against Israel have come primarily from Palestinians and those sympathetic to their cause, who may have their own axes to grind, many of these charges have also been corroborated by Israeli officials and by Israeli citizens loyal to the Jewish state. Especially noteworthy is the *Karp Report*, authored by the Deputy Attorney General of Israel, which concluded following an official inquiry that systematic miscarriage of justice has been perpetrated in the West Bank by Israeli military authorities and police (entry 151). The harshness of Israeli rule is also documented in the report by the Tel Aviv-based International Center for Peace in the Middle East (entry 152), in the book by Israeli lawyer Felicia Langer (entry 144), and in the candid account of Rafik Halabi, an Israeli Druze (entry 142).

134   Adams, Michael. "Israel's Treatment of the Arabs in the Occupied Territories." *Journal of Palestine Studies* 6 (Winter 1977), 19-40.

135   Aruri, Naseer H. "Repression in Academia: Palestinian Universities Versus the Israeli Military." *Arab Perspectives* 2 (April 1981), 14-19.

136   _____. "Resistance and Repression: Political Prisoners in Israeli Occupied Territories." *Journal of Palestine Studies* 7 (Summer 1978), 48-66.

137   Bishara, Ghassan. "The Human Rights Case Against Israel: The Policy of Torture." *Journal of Palestine Studies* 8 (Summer 1979), 3-30.

138   Cohen, Esther Rosalind. *International Criticism of Israeli Security Measures in the Occupied Territories*. Jerusalem Papers on

Peace Problems, No. 37. Jerusalem: Magnes Press, Hebrew University, 1984.

139   Curtis, Michael. "Academic Freedom and the West Bank." *Middle East Review* 15 (Spring-Summer 1983), 73-76.

140   Gerson, Allan. "State Department Reporting on Human Rights Violations: The Case of the West Bank." *Middle East Review* 13 (Winter 1980-81), 22-25.

141   Goldstein, Michael. "Israeli Security Measures in the Occupied Territories: Administrative Detention." *Middle East Journal* 32 (Winter 1978), 35-44.

142   Halabi, Rafik. *The West Bank Story*. Translated by Ina Friedman. New York: Harcourt Brace Jovanovich, 1982.

143   Jiryis, Sabri. "Domination by Law." *Journal of Palestine Studies* 11 (Autumn 1981), 67-92.

144   Langer, Felicia. *These are My Brothers: Israel and the Occupied Territories*. London: Ithaca Press, 1981.

145   Lesch, Ann M. "Israeli Deportation of Palestinians from the West Bank and the Gaza Strip, 1967-1978." *Journal of Palestine Studies* 8 (Winter 1979), 101-131.

146   _____. "Israeli Deportation of Palestinians from the West Bank and the Gaza Strip, 1967-1978. Part II." *Journal of Palestine Studies* 8 (Spring 1979), 81-112.

147   Nyang, Sulayman S. "Violation of Human Rights in the Arab Territories Occupied by Israel." *The Search: Journal of Islamic Studies* 4: 3/4 (1984), 23-40.

148   Ott, D.H. *Palestine in Perspective: Politics, Human Rights and the West Bank*. London: Quartet Books, 1980.

149   Sandler, Shmuel, and Hillel Frisch. *Israel, the Palestinians and the West Bank: A Study in Intercommunal Conflict*. Lexington, MA: Lexington Books, 1984.

150   Terry, James P. "State Terrorism: A Juridical Examination in Terms of Existing International Law." *Journal of Palestine Studies* 10 (Autumn 1980), 94-117.

151   *The Karp Report: An Israeli Government Inquiry into Settler Violence Against Palestinians on the West Bank.* Washington, D.C.: Institute for Palestine Studies, 1984.

152   Zucker, David, et al. *Research on Human Rights in the Occupied Territories, 1979-1983.* Tel Aviv: International Center for Peace in the Middle East, 1983.

Israeli Settlement Policies in the Occupied Territories

Since 1967, over 100 Israeli settlements have been established in the occupied areas, with a combined population of approximately 30,000. The apparently permanent Jewish presence in the territories has been a constant source of friction and violence between Israelis and Palestinian Arabs, and the religious-historical claims upon which many of these colonization schemes are based have seriously complicated the search for a territorial compromise that would be agreeable to all parties.

The mechanics of Israel's colonization are described by Abu-Lughod (entry 154), Davis (entry 156), Harris (entry 158), Lustick (entry 162), Newman (entry 167), Schnall (entry 168), Thorpe (entry 169), and Tillman (entry 170). The well-documented and highly acclaimed survey by Meron Benvenisti, a former Deputy-Mayor of Jerusalem, concludes that the settlement policy has led to an irreversible process of de facto annexation of the West Bank by Israel, rendering withdrawal from the area politically impossible (entry 155). This pessimistic verdict is challenged by Viorst (entry 171). The Likud party's view that the settlements enhance national security and that they are perfectly consistent with Palestinian autonomy envisioned in the Camp David accords is articulated by Israeli cabinet minister Yuval Ne'eman (entry 164).

153 Abu-Ayyash, Abdul-Ilah. "Israeli Planning Policy in the Occupied Territories." *Journal of Palestine Studies* 11 (Autumn 1981), 111-123.

154 Abu-Lughod, Janet. "Israeli Settlements in Occupied Arab Lands: Conquest to Colony." *Journal of Palestine Studies* 11 (Winter 1982), 16-54.

155 Benvenisti, Meron. *The West Bank Data Project: A Survey of Israel's Policies.* Washington, D.C.: American Enterprise Institute, 1984.

156 Davis, Uri. *The Golan Heights Under Israeli Occupation, 1967-1981.* Durham, UK: University of Durham, Center for Middle Eastern and Islamic Studies, 1983.

157 Dement, P. "Israeli Settlement Policy Today." *MERIP Reports* 13 (July-August 1983), 3-13.

158 Harris, William W. *Taking Root: Israeli Settlement in the West Bank, the Golan and Gaza-Sinai, 1967-80.* New York: Wiley, 1980.

159 Lesch, Ann M. "Israeli Settlements in the Occupied Territories." *Journal of Palestine Studies* 8 (Autumn 1978), 100-119.

160 _____. "Israeli Settlements on the West Bank: Mortgaging the Future." *Journal of South Asian and Middle East Studies* 7 (1983), 3-23.

161 Lustick, Ian. "Is Annexation a Fact?" *New Outlook* 25 (April 1982), 11-18.

162 _____. "Israel and the West Bank After Elon Moreh: The Mechanics of De Facto Annexation." *Middle East Journal* 35 (Autumn 1981), 557-577.

163 Mattar, Ibrahim. "Israeli Settlements in the West Bank and Gaza Strip." *Journal of Palestine Studies* 11 (Autumn 1981), 93-110.

164 Ne'eman, Yuval. "The Settling of Eretz Israel." *Midstream* 30 (January 1984), 7-11.

165 Negbi, M. "The Israeli Supreme Court and the Occupied Territories." *Jerusalem Quarterly*, No. 27 (Spring 1983), 33-47.

166   Newman, David. *Jewish Settlement in the West Bank: The Role of Gush Emunim.* Durham, UK: University of Durham, Center for Middle Eastern and Islamic Studies, 1982.

167   _____. "The Evolution of a Political Landscape: Geographical and Territorial Implications of Jewish Colonization in the West Bank." *Middle Eastern Studies* 21 (April 1985), 192-205.

168   Schnall, David J. *Beyond the Green Line: Israeli Settlements West of the Jordan.* New York: Praeger, 1984.

169   Thorpe, Merle, Jr., *Prescription for Conflict: Israel's West Bank Settlement Policy.* Washington, D.C.: Foundation for Middle East Peace, 1984.

170   Tillman, Seth. "The West Bank Hearings: Israel's Colonization of Occupied Territory." *Journal of Palestine Studies* 7 (Winter 1978), 71-87.

171   Viorst, Milton. "Annexation is Reversible." *American-Arab Affairs*, No. 9 (Summer 1984), 89-94.

172   Waxman, Chaim I. "American Israelis in Judea and Samaria: An Empirical Analysis." *Middle East Review* 17 (Winter 1984-85), 48-54.

173   Will, Donald S. "Ideology and Strategy of the Settlement Movement." *MERIP Reports* 10 (November-December 1980), 9-24.

174   _____. "Zionist Settlement Strategy and Its Ramifications for the Palestinian People." *Journal of Palestine Studies* 11 (Spring 1982), 37-57.

175   Zureik, Elia T. "Benvenisti's Palestine Project." *Journal of Palestine Studies* 14 (Fall 1984), 91-105.

The United States and the Palestine Conflict:

General Accounts

As noted by Tschirgi (entry 200), the U.S. became actively embroiled in the Palestine conflict long before the creation of Israel and the emergence of the Palestine refugee problem in 1948. The recently published book by Spiegel (entry 196) provides an excellent overview of American policies toward the Arab-Israeli conflict from the Truman to the Reagan administrations, and identifies the philosophies of each successive presidency as the main element shaping U.S. Middle East policy since the end of World War II. The publication of the U.S. Department of State (entry 202) contains chronologically arranged documents that present the American position on various aspects of the Arab-Israeli conflict between 1967-1983, and is therefore an indispensable reference source.

The works by Tillman (entry 198) and Chomsky (entry 181) provide the most sweeping and illuminating critiques of the American approach to the Palestine conflict. Polemical in tone yet insightful nonetheless, Chomsky develops the theme that from the late 1950s on, Washington has been committed to a Greater Israel that is expected to dominate the Middle East in the interests of American power and at the expense of Palestinian rights to self-determination. Tillman's more scholarly and balanced treatment attributes the failure of America's Middle East policy to the inability of successive administrations to reconcile four basic U.S. interests: access to oil, security of Israel, containment of the Soviet Union, and peaceful resolution of the Arab-Israeli conflict.

176   Atherton, Alfred L., Jr. "Arabs, Israelis—and Americans: A Reconsideration." *Foreign Affairs* 62 (Summer 1984), 1194-1209.

177   Bark, Dennis L., ed. *To Promote Peace: US Foreign Policy in the Middle East*. Stanford, CA: Hoover Institution Press, 1984.

178   Binder, Leonard. "Failure, Defeat, Debacle: U.S. Policy in the Middle East." *World Politics* 36 (April 1984), 437-460.

179   Brubeck, William H. *The American National Interest and Middle East Peace*. Mt. Kisco, NY: Seven Springs Center, 1981.

180   Bruzonsky, Mark A. "America's Palestinian Predicament: Fallacies and Possibilities." *International Security* 6 (Summer 1981), 93-110.

181   Chomsky, Noam. *The Fateful Triangle: The United States, Israel and the Palestinians*. Boston: South End Press, 1983.

182 Curtiss, Richard H. *A Changing Image: American Perceptions of the Arab-Israeli Dispute*. Washington, D.C.: American Educational Trust, 1982.

183 Dhanani, G. "Third Party Mediation: The Role of the U.S. in the Arab-Israeli Conflict." *India Quarterly* 38:1 (1982), 78-86.

184 Garfinkle, Adam M. " 'Common Sense' About Middle East Diplomacy: Implications for U.S. Policy in the Near Term." *Middle East Review* 17 (Winter 1984-1985), 24-32.

185 Hatfield, Mark O. "U.S. Policy in the Middle East: A Program for Failure?" *American-Arab Affairs*, No. 7 (Winter 1983-1984), 17-23.

186 Hazo, Robert G. "Conditions for Peace." *American-Arab Affairs*, No. 1 (Summer 1982), 120-126.

187 Kerr, Malcolm H. *America's Middle East Policy: Kissinger, Carter and the Future*. Beirut: Institute for Palestine Studies, 1980.

188 Kurth, James R. "U.S. Policy and the West Bank." *Middle East Review* 17 (Winter 1984-1985), 6-10.

189 Nielson, Howard C. "Examining U.S. Perceptions and Attitudes Toward the Middle East." *American-Arab Affairs*, No. 10 (Fall 1984), 9-14.

190 Reich, Bernard. "United States Middle East Policy in the Carter and Reagan Administrations." *Middle East Review* 17 (Winter 1984-1985), 12-23.

191 Said, Edward. "The U.S. and the Middle East: Recolonization or Decolonization?" *Arab Studies Quarterly* 2 (Spring 1980), 150-161.

192 Shaked, Haim, and Itamar Rabinovich, eds. *The Middle East and the U.S.* New Brunswick, NJ: Transaction Books, 1980.

193 Sicherman, Harvey. *Broker or Advocate? The U.S. Role in the Arab-Israeli Dispute, 1973-1978*. Monograph No. 25. Philadelphia: Foreign Policy Research Institute, 1978.

194 Spiegel, Steven L., ed. *American Policy in the Middle East: Where Do We Go from Here?* New York: The Josephson Research Foundation, 1983.

195 _____. "The Middle East: A Consensus of Error." *Commentary* 73 (March 1982), 15-24.

196 _____. *The Other Arab-Israeli Conflict: Making America's Middle East Policy from Truman to Reagan*. Chicago: University of Chicago Press, 1985.

197 Teslik, Kennan L. *Congress, the Executive Branch, and Special Interests: The American Response to the Arab Boycott of Israel*. Westport, CT: Greenwood, 1982.

198 Tillman, Seth. *The United States in the Middle East: Interests and Obstacles*. Bloomington: Indiana University Press, 1982.

199 Trice, Robert H. *Interest Groups and the Foreign Policy Process: U.S. Policy in the Middle East*. Beverly Hills, CA: Sage, International Studies Series, 1976.

200 Tschirgi, Dan. *The Politics of Indecision: Origins and Implications of American Involvement with the Palestine Problem*. New York: Praeger, 1983.

201 Tucker, Robert W. "Our Obsolete Middle East Policy." *Commentary* 75 (March 1983), 21-27.

202 U.S. Department of State. *The Quest for Peace: Principal United States Public Statements and Documents Relating to the Arab-Israeli Peace Process, 1967-1983*. Washington, D.C.: 1984.

203 Zurayk, Constantine. "The Palestine Question and the American Context." *Arab Studies Quarterly* 2 (Spring 1980), 127-149.

The United States and Israel

The most comprehensive analyses of the historic, religious, cultural, and political factors that have forged America's "special relationship" with Zionism and the state of Israel are found in the books by Glick (entry 208), Grose (entry 209), Reich (entries 217 and 218), and Safran (entry 220). While I.L. Kenen, the founder of the American-Israel Public Affairs Committee discusses the influence of the American Jewish community on U.S. Middle East policy from a pro-Israeli

perspective (entry 212), former Congressman Paul Findley acknowledges the strength of the Israeli lobby in Washington and accuses it of
stifling others on the opposite side of the dispute (entry 207).

The massive flow of American aid to Israel from both official and
private sources is documented by El-Khawas and Abed-Rabbo (entry
206). Supplementing this work, the studies by Ben-Zvi (entry 205),
Pollock (entry 216), and Wheelock (entry 224) all stress the point that
the vast amounts of American economic and military assistance have
given the U.S. only very limited political leverage over Israel.

204 Bahbah, Bishara A. "The United States and Israel's Energy
Security." *Journal of Palestine Studies* 11 (Winter 1982), 113-131.

205 Ben-Zvi, Abraham. *Alliance Politics and the Limits of
Influence: The Case of the US and Israel, 1975-1983* . Tel Aviv: Jaffee
Center for Strategic Studies, Tel Aviv University, 1984.

206 El-Khawas, Mohamed, and Samir Abed-Rabbo. *American Aid to
Israel: Nature and Impact.* Brattleboro, VT: Amana Books, 1984.

207 Findley, Paul. *They Dare to Speak Out: People and Institutions
Confront Israel's Lobby.* Westport, CT: Lawrence Hill, 1985.

208 Glick, Edward Bernard. *The Triangular Connection: America,
Israel, and American Jews.* Winchester, MA: Allen & Unwin, 1982.

209 Grose, Peter. *Israel in the Mind of America.* New York:Knopf,
1983.

210 Inbar, Efraim. "Sources of Tension Between Israel and the
United States." *Conflict Quarterly* (Spring 1984), 56-65.

211 _____. "The American Arms Transfer to Israel." *Middle East
Review* 25 (Fall 1982-Winter 1982/83), 40-51.

212 Kenen, I. L. *Israel's Defense Line: Her Friends and Foes in
Washington.* Buffalo: Prometheus Books, 1981.

213 McGuire, M. C. "U.S. Assistance, Israeli Allocation, and the
Arms Race in the Middle East." *Journal of Conflict Resolution* 26
(June 1982), 199-235.

214   Novik, Nimrod, ed.   *Israel in U.S. Foreign and Security Policies*. Tel Aviv: Jaffee Center for Strategic Studies, Tel Aviv University, 1984.

215   O'Brien, William V.   "Reflections on the Future of American-Israeli Relations." *Jerusalem Quarterly*, No. 22 (Winter 1982), 85-98.

216   Pollock, David.   *The Politics of Pressure: American Arms and Israeli Policy Since the Six Day War*. Westport, CT: Greenwood, 1982.

217   Reich, Bernard.   *Quest for Peace: United States-Israel Relations and the Arab-Israeli Conflict*. New Brunswick, NJ: Transaction, 1977.

218   _____.   *The United States and Israel: Influence in the Special Relationship*. New York: Praeger, 1984.

219   Rostow, Eugene V.   "The American Stake in Israel." *Commentary* 63 (April 1977), 32-46.

220   Safran, Nadav.   *Israel: The Embattled Ally*. Cambridge, MA: Harvard University Press, 1978.

221   Sicherman, Harvey.   "The United States and Israel: A Strategic Divide?" *Orbis* 24 (Summer 1980), 381-393.

222   Spiegel, Steven L.   "Israel's Economic Crisis: What the U.S. Can Do." *Commentary* 79 (April 1985), 22-28.

223   Stauffer, Thomas R.   *US Aid to Israel: The Vital Link* . Problem Paper No. 24. Washington, D.C.: Middle East Institute, 1983.

224   Wheelock, Thomas R.   "Arms for Israel: The Limit of Leverage." *International Security* 3 (Fall 1978), 123-137.

The United States and the Palestinians

The few entries under this heading reflect the fact that American policy toward the Palestinians remains a relatively unexplored topic. The book by Shadid (entry 229) examines the evolution of American-

Palestinian relations and the factors that shape them. According to Miller, U.S. policy toward the Palestinians has been influenced since 1967 by the ebb and flow of inter-Arab tensions, the Soviet-American rivalry, and constraints imposed by the American-Israel relationship (entry 227).

225 Brown, W. "The United States and the Palestinians." *International Insight* 1 (May-June 1981), 25-31.

226 Jansen, Michael E. *The United States and the Palestinian People*. Beirut: Institute for Palestine Studies, 1970.

227 Miller, Linda B. "America and the Palestinians: In Search of a Policy." In *The Palestinians and the Middle East Conflict*, pp. 281-289. Edited by Gabriel Ben-Dor. Ramat Gan, Israel: Turtledove, 1978.

228 _____. "Carter and the Palestinians." *Jerusalem Quarterly*, No. 11 (Summer 1979), 21-35.

229 Shadid, Mohammad K. *The United States and the Palestinians*. New York: St. Martin's, 1981.

American Policies and the Palestinians:

The Kissinger Years

While the U.S. was instrumental in ending the 1973 war and engineering disengagement agreements between Israel and Egypt and Israel and Syria, Secretary of State Kissinger was unable to induce any meaningful changes in Israeli policies toward the Palestinians.

Kissinger strongly defends his approach to the Arab-Israeli conflict in two autobiographical volumes (entries 238 and 239), and his policies are favorably appraised by Sheehan (entry 244). On the other hand, AlRoy (entry 230), Golan (entry 235), and Hersh (entry 236) are highly critical of Kissinger's Middle East diplomacy. The most balanced and insightful account of the formulation and substance of U.S. Middle East diplomacy during the Kissinger era can be found in Quandt's book (entry 241).

230 AlRoy, Gil Carl. *The Kissinger Experience: American Policy in the Middle East.* New York: Horizon Press, 1976.

231 Aronson, Shlomo. *Conflict and Bargaining in the Middle East: An Israeli Perspective.* Baltimore: Johns Hopkins University Press, 1978.

232 Brown, William R. *The Last Crusade: A Negotiator's Middle East Handbook.* Chicago: Nelson-Hall, 1980.

233 Feuerwenger, Marvin. *Congress and Israel: Foreign Aid Decision-Making in the House of Representatives, 1969-1976.* Westport, CT: Greenwood, 1979.

234 Ghanayem, Ishaq I., and Alden H. Voth. *The Kissinger Legacy: American Middle East Policy.* New York: Praeger, 1984.

235 Golan, Matti. *The Secret Conversations of Henry Kissinger: Step-by-Step Diplomacy in the Middle East.* Translated by Ruth G. Stern and Sol Stern. New York: Quadrangle, 1976.

236 Hersh, Seymour. *The Price of Power: Kissinger in the Nixon White House.* New York: Summit Books, 1983.

237 Kalb, Marvin, and Bernard Kalb. *Kissinger.* Boston: Little, Brown, 1979.

238 Kissinger, Henry. *White House Years.* Boston: Little, Brown, 1979.

239 _____. *Years of Upheaval.* Boston: Little, Brown, 1982.

240 Nixon, Richard. *RN: The Memoirs of Richard Nixon.* New York: Grosset & Dunlap, 1978.

241 Quandt, William B. *Decade of Decisions: American Policy Toward the Arab-Israeli Conflict, 1967-1976.* Berkeley: University of California Press, 1977.

242 Reich, Bernard. "United States Policy in the Middle East." *Current History* 70 (January 1976), 1-4.

243   Rubin, Jeffrey Z., ed. *Dynamics of Third Party Intervention: Kissinger and the Middle East.* New York: Praeger, 1981.

244   Sheehan, Edward R.F. *The Arabs, Israelis, and Kissinger: A Secret History of American Diplomacy in the Middle East.* New York: Crowell, 1976.

The Carter Years

The most significant achievement of the Carter administration's Middle East policy was the conclusion of the Camp David accords in October, 1978 (entry 258). The memoirs of Brzezinski (entry 247), Carter (entry 248), Charney (entry 249), Dayan (entry 250), Vance (entry 259) and Weizman (entry 260) shed invaluable light on the complicated negotiations process that produced the Camp David agreements. Sayegh (entry 255) provides the most succinct and detailed critique of the Camp David accords from a Palestinian perspective.

245   Ben-Zvi, Abraham. *The United States and the Palestinians: The Carter Era.* Tel Aviv: Center for Strategic Studies, Paper No. 13. Tel Aviv University, 1981.

246   Bradley, C. Paul. *The Camp David Peace Process: A Study of Carter Administration Policies 1977-80.* Grantham, NH: Tompson & Rutter, 1981.

247   Brzezinski, Zbigniew. *Power and Principle: Memoirs of the National Security Advisor, 1977-1981.* New York: Farrar, Strauss & Giroux, 1983.

248   Carter, Jimmy. *Keeping Faith: Memoirs of a President.* New York: Bantam, 1982.

249   Charney, Leon H. *Special Counsel.* New York: Philosophical Library, 1985.

250   Dayan, Moshe. *Breakthrough: A Personal Account of the Egypt-Israel Peace Negotiations.* New York: Knopf, 1981.

251   Elazar, Daniel J. *The Camp David Framework for Peace: A Shift Toward Shared Rule.* Washington, D.C.: American Enterprise Institute for Public Policy Research, 1979.

252   Haber, Eitan, et al. *The Year of the Dove.* New York: Bantam, 1979.

253   Lapidoth, Ruth. "The Camp David Agreements: Some Legal Aspects." *Jerusalem Quarterly*, No. 10 (Winter 1979), 14-27.

254   Ra'anan, Gavriel. "United States Credibility: The Carter Administration." *Middle East Review* 13 (Winter 1980-1981), 16-21.

255   Sayegh, Fayez A. "The Camp David Agreement and the Palestine Problem." *Journal of Palestine Studies* 8 (Winter 1979), 3-40.

256   Spiegel, Steven L. "The United States and the Arab-Israeli Dispute." In *Eagle Entangled: U.S. Foreign Policy in a Complex World*, pp. 336-365. Edited by Kenneth A. Oye, et al. New York: Longman, 1979.

257   Tucker, Robert W. "Behind Camp David," *Commentary* 66 (November 1978), 25-33.

258   U.S. Department of State. Bureau of Public Affairs. Office of Communication. *The Camp David Summit, September 1978.* Washington, D.C.: Government Printing Office, 1978.

259   Vance, Cyrus. *Hard Choices: Four Critical Years in American Foreign Policy.* New York: Simon & Schuster, 1983.

260   Weizman, Ezer. *The Battle for Peace.* New York: Bantam, 1981.

The Camp David Peace Process, 1979-1982

While the Camp David peace process eventually resulted in the signing of the historic Israeli-Egyptian peace treaty in March 1979 (entry 292), the two countries remained hopelessly deadlocked in the negotiations over the issue of Palestinian autonomy in the West Bank and Gaza Strip. The Camp David accords were rejected by the rest of the Arab world and the PLO from the very beginning, and on June 14, 1982,

Egypt suspended the autonomy talks because of the Israeli invasion of Lebanon. The Camp David peace process thus became moribund.

The articles by Boutros Boutros-Ghali (entry 265) and Yitzhak Shamir (entry 285) respectively outline the Egyptian and Israeli positions on the status of the occupied territories which ultimately produced irreconcilable differences between the negotiating partners. The article by Crown Prince Hassan Bin Talal of Jordan (entry 264) identifies the reasons behind the refusal of the Palestinians, Jordan, and almost all of the Arab states to join the Camp David negotiations.

261 Avineri, Shlomo. "Beyond Camp David." *Foreign Policy*, No. 46 (Spring 1982), 19-36.

262 _____. *The Continuing Peace Process in the Middle East.* Washington, D.C.: Wilson Center, International Studies Program, No. 33, 1981.

263 Ball, George W. "The Coming Crisis in Israeli-American Relations." *Foreign Affairs* 58 (Winter 1979-1980), 231-256.

264 Bin Talal, Crown Prince Hassan. "Jordan's Quest for Peace." *Foreign Affairs* 60 (Spring 1982), 802-813.

265 Boutros-Ghali, Boutros. "The Foreign Policy of Egypt in the Post-Sadat Era." *Foreign Affairs* 60 (Spring 1982), 769-788.

266 Curtis, Michael. "Three Years After Camp David." *Middle East Review* 14 (Fall 1981-Winter 1981/82), 5-14.

267 Dinstein, Yoram. "Peace Negotiations Fatigue." *Jerusalem Quarterly*, No. 11 (Spring 1979), 3-11.

268 Dowty, Alan. "In Defense of Camp David." *Commentary* 69 (April 1980), 59-68.

269 Eban, Abba. "Camp David—The Unfinished Business." *Foreign Affairs* 57 (Winter 1978-1979), 343-354.

270 Eilts, Hermann F. "A Peg-Legged Quadrille: Israel, Egypt, the U.S. and the Palestinians." *American-Arab Affairs*, No. 1 (Summer 1982), 55-66.

271 _____. "Saving Camp David: Improve the Framework." *Foreign Policy*, No. 41 (Winter 1980-1981), 3-20.

272 Freedman, Robert O., ed. *The Middle East Since Camp David.* Boulder, CO: Westview Press, 1984.

273 Ghorbal, Ashraf. "The Struggle for Peace: Where Do We Go From Here?" *American-Arab Affairs*, No. 1 (Summer 1982), 22-30.

274 Kaplowitz, Noel. "The Search for Peace in the Middle East." *International Security* 7 (Summer 1982), 181-207.

275 Lapidoth, Ruth. "The Autonomy Negotiations: A Stocktaking." *Middle East Review* 15 (Spring-Summer 1983), 35-43.

276 _____. "The Autonomy Talks." *Jerusalem Quarterly*, No. 24 (Summer 1982), 99-113.

277 Linowitz, Sol. "The Prospects for the Camp David Peace Process." *SAIS Review*, No. 2 (1981), 93-100.

278 Lustick, Ian S. "Saving Camp David: Kill the Autonomy Talks." *Foreign Policy*, No. 41 (Winter 1980-1981), 21-43.

279 Milson, Menahem. "The Palestinians and the Peace Process." *Forum* 42/43 (1981), 119-127.

280 Perlmutter, Amos. "A Race Against Time: The Egyptian-Israeli Negotiations Over the Future of Palestine." *Foreign Affairs* 57 (Summer 1979), 987-1004.

281 _____. "Dateline Israel: A New Rejectionism." *Foreign Policy*, No. 34 (Spring 1979), 165-181.

282 Reich, Bernard. "The Middle East Autonomy Talks." *Current History* 80 (January 1981), 14-17.

283 Richardson, John P. "Western Europe and the Middle East Peace Process." *American-Arab Affairs*, No. 1 (Summer 1982), 140-146.

284   Rubner, Michael. *Camp David Aftermath: Anatomy of Missed Opportunities*. Occasional Paper No. 7. Los Angeles: Center for the Study of Armament and Disarmament, California State University, 1979.

285   Shamir, Yitzhak. "Israel's Role in a Changing Middle East." *Foreign Affairs* 60 (Spring 1982), 789-801.

286   Sid-Ahmed, Mohamed. "Shifting Sands of Peace in the Middle East." *International Security* 5 (Summer 1980), 53-79.

287   U.S. Congress. House. Committee on Foreign Affairs. *An Assessment of the West Bank and Gaza Autonomy Talks, November 1980*. Hearing before the Subcommittee on Europe and the Middle East, November 21, 1980. Washington, D.C.: 1980.

288   _____. *Perspectives on the Middle East Peace Process, December 16, 1981*. Hearing before the Subcommittee on Europe and the Middle East. Washington, D.C.: 1981.

289   _____. *Status of the Middle East Peace Talks Regarding the West Bank and Gaza, October 1979*. Hearing before the Subcommittee on Europe and the Middle East, October 23, 1979. Washington, D.C.: 1979.

290   U.S. Congress. House. Committee on International Relations. *Assessment of the 1978 Middle East Camp David Agreements*. Hearing before the Subcommittee on Europe and the Middle East, September 28, 1978. Washington, D.C.: 1978.

291   U.S. Congressional Research Service. Foreign Affairs and National Defense Division. *Documents and Statements on Middle East Peace, 1979-1982*. Report prepared for the Committee on Foreign Affairs, U.S. House of Representatives. Washington, D.C.: 1982.

292   U.S. Department of State. Bureau of Public Affairs. Office of Public Communications. *The Egyptian-Israeli Peace Treaty, March 26, 1979*. Selected Documents No. 11. Washington, D.C.: April, 1979.

293   Whetten, Lawrence. "The Arab-Israeli Peace Process in the Doldrums." *World Today* 36 (August 1980), 296-304.

294   Yegnes, Tamar.   "Saudi Arabia and the Peace Process." *Jerusalem Quarterly*, No. 11 (Winter 1981), 101-120.

295   Zartman, William I.   "The Power of American Purposes." *Middle East Journal* 35 (Spring 1981), 163-177.

The Reagan Years

The complaint that the Reagan White House was initially far less concerned with the Arab-Israeli conflict than the Carter administration has been voiced by many of the studies in this section, and most notably by Robert Neumann, who had served as U.S. ambassador in several Arab capitals since 1966 (entry 312). Because it placed the Palestinian issue on the back burner, President Reagan's unsuccessful attempt in 1981 to forge an anti-Soviet "strategic consensus" that would include Israel and several of the more moderate Arab states is severely criticized by Aruri (entry 296) and Khalidi (entry 307).

A very useful but highly critical summary of the Reagan administration's approach to the Palestine issue during its first three years in office can be found in Peck's book (entry 314). The volume by Ball, et al. (entry 299) contains both a scathing critique of Reagan's Middle East policies by former Under-Secretary of State George Ball and a strong defense of these policies by former Congressman Edward Derwinski.

296   Aruri, Naseer H.   "The United States and Israel: That Very Special Relationship." *American-Arab Affairs*, No. 1 (Summer 1982), 31-42.

297   Ball, George.   "America in the Middle East: A Breakdown in Foreign Policy." *Journal of Palestine Studies* 13:3 (1984), 3-15.

298   _____.   "What Is An Ally?" *American-Arab Affairs*, No. 6 (Fall 1983), 5-14.

299   _____., et al.   *United States Policy in the Middle East*. Washington, D.C.: Georgetown University Center for Contemporary Arab Studies, 1984.

300 Bin Talal, Crown Prince Hassan. "American Policy in the Middle East: The Jordanian View." *American-Arab Affairs*, No. 9 (Summer 1984), 81-88.

301 Blitzer, Wolf. "Israel and Reagan: Looking Ahead." *SAIS Review*, No. 1 (Winter 1981), 121-128.

302 Fabian, Larry L. "The Middle East: War Dangers and Receding Peace Prospects." *Foreign Affairs* 62:3 (1984), 632-658.

303 Foreign Policy Association. *Israel and the U.S.: Friendship and Discord*. Washington, D.C.: Foreign Policy Association, 1984.

304 Garfinkle, Adam. "U.S.-Israeli Relations: The Wolf This Time?" *Orbis* 26:1 (1982), 11-19.

305 Kehrer, W. "U.S. Funding for the Israeli Lavi Project: An Examination and Analysis." *Middle East Insight* 3 (November-December 1984), 9-17.

306 Kellum, A. "U.S.-Israeli Relations: A Reassessment." *Link* 15 (December 1982), 1-12.

307 Khalidi, Walid. "Regiopolitics: Toward a U.S. Policy on the Palestine Problem." *Foreign Affairs* 59 (Summer 1981), 1050-1063.

308 Khouri, Fred J. "The Challenge to U.S. Security and Middle East Policy." *American-Arab Affairs*, No. 5 (Summer 1983), 10-20.

309 Lawson, F. "The Reagan Administration in the Middle East." *MERIP Reports*, No. 128 (November-December 1984), 27-34.

310 Lendenmann, G. Neal. "The Struggle in Congress Over Aid Levels to Israel." *American-Arab Affairs*, No. 3 (Winter 1982-1983), 83-93.

311 Murphy, Richard W. "The Response from the United States to Current Political Developments in the Middle East." *American-Arab Affairs*, No. 8 (Spring 1984), 8-12.

312 Neumann, Robert G. "The Search for Peace in the Middle East: A Role for U.S. Policy." *American-Arab Affairs*, No. 1 (Summer 1982), 3-12.

313 _____. "Toward a Reagan Middle East Policy?" *Orbis* 25:3 (1981), 491-496.

314 Peck, Juliana. *The Reagan Administration and the Palestine Question: The First Thousand Days*. Washington, D.C.: Institute for Palestine Studies, 1984.

315 Perlmutter, Amos. "American Policy in the Middle East: New Approaches for a New Administration." *Parameters* 11:2 (1981), 14-18.

316 _____. "Reagan's Middle East Policy." *Orbis* 26:1 (1982), 26-29.

317 Razin, A. "US Foreign Aid to Israel." *Jerusalem Quarterly*, No. 29 (Fall 1983), 11-19.

318 Rubenberg, Cheryl A. "The Conduct of U.S. Foreign Policy in the Middle East in the 1983-84 Presidential Election Season." *American-Arab Affairs*, No. 9 (Summer 1984), 22-45.

319 Seelye, Talcott W. "U.S.-Syrian Relations: The Thread of Mu'awiyah." *American-Arab Affairs*, No. 4 (Spring 1983), 40-45.

320 Segal, H. "The United States and Israel—An Ambiguous Support." *International Insight* 1 (May-June 1981), 19-24.

321 Sisco, Joseph J. "Middle East: Progress or Lost Opportunity?" *Foreign Affairs* 61:3 (1983), 611-640.

322 Sterner, Michael. "Managing U.S.-Israeli Relations." *American-Arab Affairs*, No. 6 (Fall 1983), 15-23.

323 Tillman, Seth P. "U.S. Middle East Policy: Theory and Practice." *American-Arab Affairs*, No. 4 (Spring 1983), 1-11.

324 Tucker, Robert. "The Middle East: Carterism Without Carter?" *Commentary* 72 (September 1981), 27-36.

325 U.S. Congress. House. Committee on Foreign Affairs. *Developments in the Middle East, February 1982*. Hearings before the Subcommittee on Europe and the Middle East, February 8, 1982. Washington, D.C.: 1982.

326 _____. *Developments in the Middle East, March 1984*. Hearing before the Subcommittee on Europe and the Middle East, March 21, 1984. Washington, D.C.: 1984.

327 Wright, Claudia. "Reagan Arms Policy, the Arabs and Israel: Protectorate or Protection Racket?" *Third World Quarterly* 6 (July 1984), 638-656.

328 _____. "Shadow on Sand: Strategy and Deception in Reagan's Policy Toward the Arabs." *Journal of Palestine Studies* 11 (Spring 1982), 3-36.

Strategic Cooperation Agreement with Israel

In November 1981, the U.S. and Israel initialed a strategic cooperation memorandum of understanding that called for joint military maneuvers, transfer of advanced military technology developed in the U.S. to Israel, Israeli arms sales to U.S. forces in the Middle East, stockpiling of American medical supplies in Israel, exchanges of intelligence, and joint security planning. Following Israel's annexation of the Golan Heights in December 1981, Washington suspended the negotiations on the strategic cooperation accord. The talks eventually resumed, and in November 1983, the two governments agreed to implement the joint undertaking.

Hameed (entry 333) articulates the widely-held argument that the strategic cooperation accord removes any significant incentive for Israel to compromise on the West Bank and seriously jeopardizes America's role as an impartial arbitrator in the Israeli-Palestinian conflict. Echoing the same concerns, Green (entry 332) also maintains that the agreement has hastened the very Soviet penetration into the Middle East which had induced the U.S. to cooperate with Israel in the first place. Recognizing the political costs, Adams (entry 329) concludes that Israel offers clear and substantial advantages as a prepositioning site for U.S. projection forces in the region.

329 Adams, Jay. "Assessing Israel As a 'Strategic Asset': A Quantitative Comparison with Other Prepositioning Sites." *Middle East Review* 14 (Fall 1981-Winter 1981/82), 43-54.

330 Bryen, S. "Advancing US-Israeli Strategic Cooperation." *Middle East Review (Special Report)* 4 (February 1984), 1-7.

331 Campbell, John C. "The Security Factor in U.S. Middle East Policy." *American-Arab Affairs*, No. 5 (Summer 1983), 1-9.

332 Green, Stephen. "Strategic Asset, Soviet Opportunity." *American-Arab Affairs*, No. 9 (Summer 1984), 46-54.

333 Hameed, Mazher. "The Impact and Implications of the U.S.-Israeli Strategic Cooperation Agreement." *American-Arab Affairs*, No. 8 (Spring 1984), 13-19.

334 Spiegel, Steven L. "Israel As a Strategic Asset." *Commentary* 75 (June 1983), 51-55.

The September 1982 Peace Initiative

In September 1982, President Reagan unveiled his peace plan for the Middle East (entry 354). Explicitly rejecting both, Israeli annexation of the occupied territories and the creation of an independent Palestinian state in the West Bank and Gaza, it envisioned full Palestinian autonomy in these areas in association with Jordan. The peace initiative also called for an immediate settlement freeze by Israel and urged the Arab states to recognize Israel's existence and to negotiate with it directly about all outstanding issues, including the final status of Jerusalem. Unfortunately, these proposals were rejected by the Likud-led Israeli government, by most Arab states, and by the PLO.

The monograph by Aruri, et al. (entry 338) contains three articles that examine the objectives, substance and implications of the Reagan plan. The Palestinian reaction to the peace initiative is analyzed by Nakhleh (entry 351). While Dawisha claims that the Reagan proposal is superior to the Camp David plan because it accommodates the requirements of a potentially successful bargaining process (entry 341), both former President Carter (entry 347) and Hakki (entry 346) lament the Reagan administration's failure to pursue its peace plan more vigorously.

335 Alireza, Abdullah A. "An Arab View of the Peace Process." *American-Arab Affairs*, No. 4 (Spring 1983), 70-76.

336   Aruri, Naseer H. "The Reagan Mideast Initiative: Short Change and Traps." *Arab Student Journal* 4 (October/November/December 1982), 25-31.

337   _____, and Fouad Moughrabi. "The Reagan Middle East Initiative." *Journal of Palestine Studies* 12 (Winter 1983), 10-30.

338   _____, Fouad Moughrabi, and Joe Stork. *Reagan and the Middle East.* Belmont, MA: AAUG Press, 1983.

339   Azar, Edward. "United States Foreign Policy Options in the Middle East." *Arab Perspective* 3 (May 1983), 5-20.

340   Campbell, John C. *The Reagan Plan and the Western Alliance.* Washington, D.C.: Center for Middle East Policy, 1983.

341   Dawisha, Adeed. "Comprehensive Peace in the Middle East and the Comprehension of Arab Politics." *Middle East Journal* 37 (Winter 1983), 43-53.

342   Eilts, Hermann F. "President Reagan's Middle East Peace Initiative." *American-Arab Affairs*, No. 2 (Fall 1982), 1-5.

343   Fabian, Larry L. "The Red Light." *Foreign Policy*, No. 50 (Spring 1983), 53-72.

344   Faksh, Mahmud A. "The Chimera of Peace in the Middle East." *American-Arab Affairs*, No. 2 (Fall 1982), 26-32.

345   Guiney, A. "The Reagan Plan: An Evaluation." *New Outlook* 26 (January-February 1983), 18-21.

346   Hakki, Mohamed I. "U.S.-Egyptian Relations." *American-Arab Affairs*, No. 6 (Fall 1983), 28-33.

347   "Interview with Jimmy Carter." *American-Arab Affairs*, No. 7 (Winter 1983-84), 1-10.

348   Kipper, Judith. "President Reagan Takes the Lead." *American-Arab Affairs*, No. 2 (Fall 1982), 15-18.

349   Kreczko, Alan J. "Support Reagan's Initiative." *Foreign Policy*, No. 49 (Winter 1982-83), 140-153.

350 Lustick, Ian S. "Israeli Politics and American Foreign Policy." *Foreign Affairs* 61 (Winter 1982/83), 379-399.

351 Nakhleh, Emile A. "A 'Fresh Start' Toward Peace." *American-Arab Affairs*, No. 2 (Fall 1982), 6-10.

352 Neumann, Robert. "Finally—A U.S. Middle East Policy." *Washington Quarterly* 6:2 (1983), 199-208.

353 Ramati, Yohanan. "The Reagan Plan." *Midstream* 29 (March 1983), 3-6.

354 Reagan, Ronald. "A New Opportunity for Peace in the Middle East." Address to the Nation, September 1, 1982. *American-Arab Affairs*, No. 2 (Fall 1982), 149-154.

355 Schenker, H. "The Reagan Initiative and Israel." *Jewish Frontier* 49 (October 1982), 4-5.

356 Taylor, Alan R. "The Crucial Test for U.S. Policy." *American-Arab Affairs*, No. 2 (Fall 1982), 11-14.

357 U.S. Congress. House. Committee on Foreign Affairs. *The Unfinished Business of the Peace Process in the Middle East.* Report of a Study Mission to Israel, Jordan, Saudi Arabia, Lebanon, Syria, France, and England, November 6-20, 1982, for the Subcommittee on Europe and the Middle East, January 25, 1983. Washington, D.C.: 1983.

The Israeli Invasion of Lebanon:

Background and Causes

In early June 1982, the Israel Defense Forces (IDF) invaded Lebanon, ostensibly in order to silence PLO artillery in Southern Lebanon that had been shelling Israeli settlements in the Northern Galilee. However, as the invasion escalated to a full-fledged war, it became increasingly clear that Israeli objectives went well beyond the mere establishment of a 25-mile *cordon sanitaire* in South Lebanon. In the most comprehensive, authoritative, and critical account of the war, Schiff and Ya'ari (entry 371) argue persuasively that Israel invaded its northern neighbor in order to expel the PLO and evict Syrian forces from Lebanon, install a Christian-dominated regime in Beirut that would eventually sign a peace treaty with Israel, and impose a *Pax Israeliana* in the West Bank after decimating the PLO infrastructure in Lebanon.

The volumes by Jansen (entry 361) and Rabinovich (entry 365) provide useful background to the events that culminated in the Israeli decision to invade Lebanon. Classified documents seized at PLO headquarters in Sidon provide documentation that the PLO had created a mini-state in South Lebanon and had amassed vast military stockpiles for an eventual war against Israel (entry 360). While the Mallisons argue that the invasion was an act of unprovoked aggression against the PLO and the republic of Lebanon under existing rules of international law (entry 362), O'Brien (entry 364) and Tucker (entry 372) justify the Israeli attack as the continuation of a war of legitimate self-defense that has been in progress ever since the formation of the PLO in 1964.

358 Abu-Lughod, Ibrahim, and Eqbal Ahmad. *The Invasion of Lebanon*. London: Institute of Race Relations, 1983.

359 Akins, James E. "The Flawed Rationale for Israel's Invasion of Lebanon." *American-Arab Affairs*, No. 2 (Fall 1982), 32-39.

360 Israeli, Raphael, ed. *PLO in Lebanon: Selected Documents*. New York: St. Martin's, 1984.

361 Jansen, Michael. *The Battle of Beirut: Why Israel Invaded Lebanon*. Westport, CT: Lawrence Hill, 1982.

362 Mallison, Sally V., and W. Thomas Mallison. "Israel in Lebanon, 1982: Aggression or Self-Defense?" *American-Arab Affairs*, No. 5 (Summer 1983), 39-49.

363 Nakhleh, K. "The Invasion of Lebanon and Israel's Imperial Strategy." *Arab Studies Quarterly* 4:4 (1982), 324-336.

364 O'Brien, William V. "Israel in Lebanon." *Middle East Review* 15 (Fall 1982-Winter 1982/83), 5-14.

365 Rabinovich, Itamar. *The War for Lebanon, 1970-1983*. Ithaca, NY: Cornell University Press, 1984.

366 Rubenberg, Cheryl A. "The Civilian Infrastructure of the Palestine Liberation Organization: An Analysis of the PLO in Lebanon until June 1982." *Journal of Palestine Studies* 12 (Spring 1983), 54-78.

367 _____. "The Israeli Invasion of Lebanon: Objectives and Consequences." *Journal of South Asian and Middle East Studies* 8:2 (1984), 3-29.

368 Ryan, Sheila. "Israel's Invasion of Lebanon: Background to the Crisis." *Journal of Palestine Studies* 11-12 (Summer/Fall 1982), 23-37.

369 Schiff, Zeev. "Lebanon: Motivations and Interests in Israel's Policy." *Middle East Journal* 38 (Spring 1984), 220-227.

370 _____, and Hirsh Goodman. "The Road to War: Ariel Sharon's Modern Day 'Putsch'." *Spectrum* 2 (April-May 1984), 8-13.

371 _____, and Ehud Ya'ari. *Israel's Lebanon War.* Edited and translated by Ina Friedman. New York: Simon & Schuster, 1984.

372 Tucker, Robert W. "Lebanon: The Case for the War." *Commentary* 74 (October 1982), 19-30.

373 Wurmser, D. "Egypto-Centrism in Israeli Strategic Planning: The 'Peace for Galilee' Operation." *SAIS Review* 4 (Summer-Fall 1984), 65-76.

374 Yaniv, Avner. "Moral Fervor vs. Strategic Logic: A Note on the Rationale of the Israeli Invasion of Lebanon." *Middle East Review* 15 (Spring/Summer 1983), 5-10.

375 _____, and Robert Lieber. "Personal Whim or Strategic Imperative? The Israeli Invasion of Lebanon." *International Security* 8:2 (1983), 117-142.

The Course of the War

After capturing South Lebanon, Israeli forces advanced rapidly to the North and East, eventually clashed with Syrian troops in the Bekaa Valley, entered Beirut, and laid a merciless siege against its Western, Moslem-dominated sector. Although the invasion was initially supposed to have ended in a matter of days, it took Israel approximately three years to withdraw its forces and to extricate itself from the Lebanese quagmire.

In addition to the previously-noted volume by Schiff and Ya'ari (entry 371), the books by Bulloch (entry 378), Gabriel (entry 381) and Randal (entry 386) provide extensive information on the military and political aspects of the war. The devastating two-month siege of Beirut is covered in the works by Clifton and Leroy (entry 379), Mikadadi (entry 383), Nassib (entry 384) and Rubenberg (entry 387), all of which were written by eyewitnesses. Harsh indictments of IDF brutality against Lebanese civilians and Palestinians can be found in the vivid accounts of Timerman, the well-known Jewish human rights activist who had immigrated to Israel shortly before the war (entry 390), and in the book by Yermiya, a Lieutenant Colonel in the IDF who was assigned to civilian relief in the wake of the invasion (entry 392).

376 Bavly, Dan, and Eliahu Salpeter. *Fire in Beirut: Israel's War in Lebanon with the PLO*. New York: Stein & Day, 1984.

377 Bloom, James J. "The Six-Days-Plus-Ten Weeks War: Aspects of Israel's Summer Campaign in Lebanon, 1982." *Middle East Insight* 2 (January-February 1983), 45-55.

378 Bulloch, John. *Final Conflict: The War in Lebanon*. London: Century, 1983.

379 Clifton, Tony., and Catherine Leroy. *God Cried*. New York: Quartet Books, 1983.

380 Danaher, Kevin. "Israel's use of Cluster Bombs in Lebanon." *Journal of Palestine Studies* 11-12 (Summer/Fall 1982), 48-57.

381 Gabriel, Richard A. *Operation Peace for Galilee: The Israel-PLO War in Lebanon*. New York: Hill & Wang, 1984.

382 MacBride, Sean, et al. *Israel in Lebanon: The Report of the International Commission*. London: Ithaca Press, 1983.

383 Mikadadi, Lina. *Surviving the Siege of Beirut: A Personal Account*. London: Onyx Press, 1983.

384   Nassib, Salim. *Beirut: Frontline Story.* London: Pluto Press, 1983.

385   Perlmutter, Amos. "Begin's Rhetoric and Sharon's Tactics." *Foreign Affairs* 61 (Fall 1982), 67-83.

386   Randal, Jonathan C. *Going All the Way: Christian Warlords, Israeli Adventurers and the War in Lebanon.* New York: Viking Press, 1983.

387   Rubenberg, Cheryl. "Eyewitness: Beirut Under Fire." *Journal of Palestine Studies* 11-12 (Summer/Fall 1982), 62-68.

388   Sahliyeh, Emile. *The Lebanon War.* Boulder, CO: Westview, 1985.

389   Sayigh, Yezid. "Palestinian Military Performance in the 1982 War." *Journal of Palestine Studies* 12 (Spring 1983), 3-24.

390   Timerman, Jacobo. *The Longest War: Israel in Lebanon.* Translated by Miguel Acoca. New York: Knopf, 1982.

391   Wright, Clifford A. "The Israeli War Machine in Lebanon." *Journal of Palestine Studies* 12 (Winter 1983), 38-53.

392   Yermiya, Dov. *My War Diary: Lebanon, June 5 - July 1, 1982.* Translated by Hillel Schenker. Boston: South End Press, 1983.

The Sabra and Shatila Massacres

The siege of Beirut tragically culminated in the systematic slaughter of hundreds of Palestinians by armed Christian Phalange forces who had entered the Sabra and Shatila camps with the apparent acquiescence of Israeli Defense Minister Sharon and several top commanders of the IDF. The events that led up to the massacre are chronicled by Kapeliouk, who is an Israeli-born journalist now living in France (entry 395). Al-Sheikh, a Palestinian who was brought up in the Shatila camp, provides an eyewitness account of the massacre (entry 396).

In response to both international condemnation and mass protests inside Israel, the Begin government appointed an official commission of inquiry to investigate Israel's role in the massacre. The Kahan Commission report was eventually released in February 1983 (entry 397), and it recommended dismissal and/or censure of several top military officers, including Defense Minister Sharon. Sharon resigned but later accepted Mr. Begin's offer to remain in the Cabinet as minister without portfolio. The findings of the Kahan report, which absolved Israel from direct responsibility for the tragedy, are severely criticized by Ahmad for their failure to disclose all the known facts (entry 393).

393 Ahmad, Eqbal . "The Public Relations of Ethnocide." *Journal of Palestine Studies* 12 (Spring 1983), 31-40.

394 Genet, Jean. "Four Hours in Shatila." *Journal of Palestine Studies* 12 (Spring 1983), 3-22.

395 Kapeliouk, Amnon. *Sabra and Shatila: Inquiry into a Massacre.* Belmont, MA: Association of Arab-American University Graduates, 1984.

396 Al-Sheikh, Zakaria. "Sabra and Shatila 1982: Resisting the Massacre." *Journal of Palestine Studies* 14 (Fall 1984), 57-90.

397 *The Beirut Massacre: The Complete Kahan Commission Report.* Introduced by Abba Eban. New York: Karz-Cohl, 1983.

United States' Involvement

According to Schiff (entry 409) and several other studies cited in this section, former Secretary of State Haig gave Israel a "green light" for the invasion in early 1982. The U.S. then became more directly involved in the Lebanese imbroglio when it helped to arrange withdrawal of Palestinian, Syrian and Israeli troops from West Beirut in August 1982. Eventually, 800 U.S. Marines participated in the multinational peacekeeping force that supervised the departure of PLO fighters from Beirut (entry 405). Following the Sabra and Shatila massacre, the Marines returned to Beirut as part of an expanded international peacekeeping force in September 1982 (entries 413 and 414).

According to both former ambassador Hermann Eilts (entry 400), and former NSC staff member William Quandt (entry 406), the Reagan administration ran into deep troubles when the U.S. Marine contingent ceased to operate as an impartial peacekeeping force and actively assisted the Gemayel government against its domestic rivals. While the U.S. managed to secure in May 1983 Lebanese and Israeli approval of an agreement calling for the withdrawal of all foreign troops, American failure to include Syria in the negotiations resulted in the rejection of the accord by Syria and the eventual abrogation of the agreement by Lebanon in early 1984. In the wake of the diplomatic impasse and following the loss of 264 Marines, President Reagan ordered the departure of American forces from Lebanese soil in February 1984.

398   Ball, George W. *Error and Betrayal in Lebanon.* Washington, D.C.: Foundation for Middle East Peace, 1984.

399   Binder, Leonard. "Operation Bootstrap: The Logic of American Strategy in Lebanon." *Middle East Insight* 2:4 (1982), 11-17.

400   Eilts, Hermann F. "Standing Small in the Middle East." *Middle East Insight* 3 (April-May 1984), 3-11.

401   Mallison, Sally V., and W. Thomas Mallison. "The United States and Israeli Violations of Law." *Journal of Palestine Studies* 11-12 (Summer/Fall 1982), 58-61.

402   Muir, Jim. "Lebanon: Arena of Conflict, Crucible of Peace." *Middle East Journal* 38 (Spring 1984), 204-219.

403   Orfalea, G. "How the U.S. Helps Israel Destroy Lebanon." *Arab Perspectives* 3 (March 1982), 12-17.

404   Pipes, Daniel. "'Death to America' in Lebanon." *Middle East Insight* 4 (March-April 1985), 3-9.

405   "Plan for PLO Departure and Exchange of Notes Between the Governments of the U.S. and Lebanon, Announced August 20, 1982." *American-Arab Affairs*, No. 2 (Fall 1982), 139-148.

406   Quandt, William B. "Reagan's Lebanon Policy: Trial and Error." *Middle East Journal* 38 (Spring 1984), 237-254.

407   Rahall, Nick J. "Lebanon and U.S. Foreign Policy Toward the Middle East." *American-Arab Affairs*, No. 2 (Fall 1982), 40-50.

408 Schiff, Zeev. "Dealing with Syria." *Foreign Policy*, No. 55 (Summer 1984), 92-112.

409 ____. "The Green Light." *Foreign Policy*, No. 50 (Spring 1983), 73-85.

410 Snider, Lewis W. *The Lebanese Crisis, the Lebanese Forces, and the American Foreign Policy*. Santa Monica, CA: California Seminar on International Security and Foreign Policy, 1984.

411 U.S. Congress. House. Committee on Armed Services. *The Use of U.S. Military Personnel in Lebanon and Consideration of Report from Sept. 24-25 Committee Delegation to Lebanon*. Hearings, September 27-28, 1983. Washington, D.C.: 1984.

412 ____. Committee on Foreign Affairs. *Developments in Lebanon and the Middle East, January 1984*. Hearing before the Subcommittee on Europe and the Middle East, January 26, 1984. Washington, D.C.: 1984.

413 ____. *Multinational Force in Lebanon Resolution* . Report to Accompany H.J.Res. 364, September 27, 1983. Washington, D.C.: 1983.

414 ____. *Statutory Authorization Under the War Powers Resolution: Lebanon*. Hearing and Markup on H.J.Res. 364 and H.Res. 315, September 21-22, 1983. Washington, D.C.: 1983.

415 ____. *The Crisis in Lebanon: U.S. Policy and Alternative Legislative Proposals*. Hearings, February 1-2, 1984. Washington, D.C.: 1984.

416 ____. *The Situation in Lebanon: U.S. Role in the Middle East*. Hearing, September 9, 1982. Washington, D.C.: 1982.

417 ____. Senate. Armed Services Committee. *The Situation in Lebanon*. Hearings, October 25-31, 1983. Washington, D.C.: 1984.

418 ____. Committee on Foreign Relations. *Authorization for U.S. Marines in Lebanon*. Hearings, November 10-15, 1983. Washington, D.C.: 1984.

419 _____. *Events in Lebanon.* Hearing, September 13, 1983. Washington, D.C.: 1983.

420 _____. *Policy Options in Lebanon* . Hearing, January 11, 1984. Washington, D.C.: 1984.

421 _____. *Situation in Lebanon.* Hearing, December 1, 1982. Washington, D.C.: 1983.

422 Wright, Claudia. "The Turn of the Screw—The Lebanon War and American Policy." *Journal of Palestine Studies* 11-12 (Summer/Fall 1982), 3-22.

Consequences and Implications

The 1982 Israeli-Lebanese war ended in disaster for all parties involved in the conflict. Ajami (entry 424) and Faksh (entry 429) emphasize that the war contributed to Lebanon's further political disintegration, while Nakhleh and Wright (entry 437) argue that American goals in the Middle East were dealt a severe setback.

According to Cohen (entry 427), Israel managed to destroy the PLO's "state within a state" in Southern Lebanon, but Schiff and Ya'ari (entry 371) echo the dominant view that the war ended in debacle for Israel because it did not eradicate Palestinian presence in the South, failed to drive the Syrians out, did not create a viable and pro-Israeli Maronite regime in Beirut, and exacerbated strife between Israel and the Palestinians. The articles by Norton (entries 439, 440 and 441) focus on the severe difficulties experienced by Israel as it began extricating itself from Lebanon, and Yishai notes that Israel was wracked by unprecedented internal dissent over the goals, strategies and tactics of the war (entry 449).

423 Abu-Lughod, Ibrahim. "The Meaning of Beirut, 1982." *Race and Class* 24 (Spring 1983), 345-359.

424 Ajami, Fouad. "Lebanon and its Inheritors." *Foreign Affairs* 63 (Spring 1985), 778-799.

425 _____. "The Shadows of Hell." *Foreign Policy* No. 48 (Fall 1982), 94-110.

426 Alpher, Joseph., ed. *Israel's Lebanon Policy: Where to?* Tel Aviv: Jaffee Center for Strategic Studies, Tel Aviv University, 1984.

427 Cohen, Eliot A. "'Peace for Galilee': Success or Failure?" *Commentary* 78 (November 1984), 24-30.

428 Davidson, Larry. "Lebanon and the Jewish Conscience." *Journal of Palestine Studies* 12 (Winter 1983), 54-60.

429 Faksh, Mahmud A. "Lebanon: The Road to Disintegration." *American-Arab Affairs*, No. 8 (Spring 1984), 20-30.

430 Frankel, J. "Israel: The War and After." *Dissent* 30 (Winter 1983), 7-14.

431 Gabriel, Richard A. "Lessons of the War: The IDF in Lebanon." *Military Review* 64 (August 1984), 47-65.

432 Gemayel, Amine. "The Price and the Promise." *Foreign Affairs* 63 (Spring 1985), 759-777.

433 Khoury, E., and N. Housepian. "Israel's Future in Lebanon." *MERIP Reports* 12 (September-October 1982), 28-32.

434 Korany, B. "The Cold Peace, the Sixth Arab-Israeli War, and Egypt's Public." *International Journal* 38:4 (1983), 652-673.

435 Ledeen, Michael. "The Lessons of Lebanon." *Commentary* 77 (May 1984), 15-22.

436 Ma'oz, Moshe. "Israel and the Arabs After the Lebanese War." *Jerusalem Quarterly*, No. 28 (Summer 1983), 25-34.

437 Nakhleh, Khalil, and Clifford A. Wright. *After the Palestine-Israel War: Limits to U.S. and Israeli Policy.* Belmont, MA: Institute of Arab Studies, 1983.

438 Neumann, Robert G. "Assad and the Future of the Middle East." *Foreign Affairs* 62 (Winter 1983/84), 237-256.

439 Norton, Augustus R. "Israel and South Lebanon." *American-Arab Affairs*, No. 4 (Spring 1983), 23-31.

440 _____. "Making Enemies in South Lebanon: Harakat Amal, the IDF, and South Lebanon." *Middle East Insight* 3 (January-February 1984), 13-20.

441 _____. "Occuaptional Risks and Planned Retirement: The Israeli Withdrawal from South Lebanon." *Middle East Insight* 4 (March-April 1985), 14-18.

442 Ober, Ralph. "The Lebanese Campaign in Retrospect." *Midstream* 29 (March 1983), 7-12.

443 Raab, Earl. "How American Jews Have Reacted to the War." *Jewish Monthly* 97 (August-September 1982), 40-44.

444 Saunders, Harold H. "An Israeli-Palestinian Peace." *Foreign Affairs* 61 (Fall 1982), 101-121.

445 Sayigh, Rosemary. "The *Mulchabarat* State: A Palestinian Woman's Testimony." *Journal of Palestine Studies* 14 (Spring 1985), 18-31.

446 Schenker, Hillel., ed. *After Lebanon: The Israeli-Palestinian Connection.* New York: Pilgrim Press, 1983.

447 Seliktar, Ofira. "The New Zionism." *Foreign Policy*, No. 51 (Summer 1983), 118-138.

448 Yaari, Ehud. "Israel's Dilemma in Lebanon." *Middle East Insight* 3 (April-May 1984), 18-23.

449 Yishai, Yael. "Dissent in Israel: Opinions on the Lebanon War." *Middle East Review* 16 (Winter 1983-1984), 38-44.

The Palestinians in the Aftermath of the Lebanese War

The 1982 war shattered the PLO's conventional military capabilities and approximately 6,000 Palestinian fighters were compelled to leave Beirut and were dispersed in Syria, Algeria, Tunisia, Jordan, Iraq, and North and South Yemen. In February 1983, the Palestine National Council rejected President Reagan's 1982 peace plan but approved the concept of a confederation between Jordan and an independent Palestinian state (entries 450 and 471).

Opposed to the rapprochement between Yasser Arafat and King Hussein of Jordan, Syrian-backed anti-Arafat factions within the PLO and Al-Fatah initiated a rebellion against Arafat loyalists in Lebanon in May 1983. The events that culminated in Arafat's expulsion from Syria and the evacuation of his forces from Tripoli in late 1983 are covered by Garfinkle (entry 455), Kanin (entry 458) and Khalidi (entry 459).

In December 1983, Arafat restored PLO-Egyptian relations and, despite the boycott of Syrian-supported dissidents, continued the dialogue with Jordan throughout 1984 in search of a political solution to the Palestine problem. The eventual Hussein-Arafat agreement calling for an international peace conference that would include a joint Jordanian-Palestinian delegation, and leaving open the possibility of a Jordanian-Palestinian confederation, has been rejected by Syria and by the more extreme factions of the PLO.

These developments lend further proof to Miller's contention that the 1982 war left the PLO without an independent base of operations, with greater internal disarray than ever before, and without an effective political and military strategy against Israel (entry 464).

450   Abu-Lughod, Ibrahim. "Flexible Militancy: A Report on the Sixteenth Session of the Palestine National Council, Algiers, February 14-22, 1983." *Journal of Palestine Studies* 12 (Summer 1983), 25-40.

451   Ahmad, Eqbal. "Yasser Arafat's Nightmare." *MERIP Reports* 13 (November-December 1983), 18-23.

452   Aruri, Naseer H. "Palestinian Nationalism After Lebanon: The Current Impasse." *American-Arab Affairs*, No. 8 (Spring 1984), 54-65.

453   _____. "The PLO and the Jordan Option." *MERIP Reports*, No. 131 (March-April 1985), 3-9.

454   Eytan, Z. "The Palestinian Armed Forces After Beirut." *Jerusalem Quarterly*, No. 32 (Summer 1984), 131-139.

455   Garfinkle, Adam. "Sources of the Al-Fatah Mutiny." *Orbis* 27:3 (1983), 603-640.

456   Hudson, Michael. "The Palestinians After Lebanon." *Current History* 82 (January 1983), 5-9, 34.

457   _____. "The Palestinians After Lebanon."   *Current History* 84 (January 1985), 16-20.

458   Kanin, J. "The PLO in the Aftermath of Rebellion." *SAIS Review* 5:1 (1985), 91-107.

459   Khalidi, Rashid.   "Behind the Fatah Rebellion." *MERIP Reports* 13 (November-December 1983), 6-12.

460   _____. "The Assad Regime and the Palestinian Resistance." *Arab Studies Quarterly* 6 (Fall 1984), 259-266.

461   _____. "The Palestinians in Lebanon: Social Repercussions of Israel's Invasion." *Middle East Journal* 38 (Spring 1984), 255-266.

462   Miller, Aaron D. "Illusion and Reality." *Jerusalem Quarterly*, No. 31 (Spring 1984), 58-63.

463   _____. "Syria and the Arab-Israeli Conflict: The Palestinian Factor." *Middle East Insight* 4 (June-July 1985), 3-9.

464   _____. "The Future of Palestinian Nationalism." *Middle East Insight* 3 (July-August 1984), 23-29.

465   _____. "The PLO After Tripoli: The Arab Dimension." *American-Arab Affairs*, No. 8 (Spring 1984), 66-73.

466   _____. "The PLO: What Next?" *Washington Quarterly* 6 (Winter 1983), 116-125.

467   _____. "Whither the PLO?" *Middle East Review* 16 (Spring 1984), 40-43.

468   Moughrabi, Fouad. "The Palestinians After Lebanon." *Arab Studies Quarterly* 5:3 (1983), 211-219.

469   Pipes, Daniel. "How Important Is the PLO?" *Commentary* 75 (April 1983), 17-25.

470 Rouleau, Eric. "The Future of the PLO." *Foreign Affairs* 62 (Fall 1983), 138-156.

471 Rubenberg, Cheryl A. "The PLO Response to the Reagan Initiative: The PNC at Algiers, February 1983." *American-Arab Affairs*, No. 4 (Spring 1983), 53-69.

472 Said, Edward W. "Palestinians in the Aftermath of Beirut." *Journal of Palestine Studies* 12 (Winter 1983), 3-9.

473 _____. "Palestinians in the Aftermath of Beirut: A Preliminary Stocktaking." *Arab Studies Quarterly* 4:4 (1982), 301-308.

474 Seale, P. "PLO Strategies: Algiers and After." *World Today* 39 (April 1983), 137-144.

475 Stein, Kenneth W. "The PLO After Beirut." *Middle East Review* 15 (Spring-Summer 1983), 11-17.

The Palestinian Conflict and the Question of Jerusalem

Shortly after the end of the 1967 war, Israel formally annexed East Jerusalem, an area that had been under Jordanian rule since 1948 and which contains the Western Wall, the holiest shrine in Judaism. While successive Israeli governments have vowed to retain a unified Jerusalem as Israel's eternal capital, the international community has not recognized the legality of Israeli claims over the entire city, and vast majorities in the U.N., the Arab states, and the PLO have demanded Israeli withdrawal from the city's Eastern sector. Prospects for a peaceful solution of the Arab-Israeli conflict remain dim as long as the status of Jerusalem, a city that also includes many Islamic and Christian holy places, remains unresolved.

Yishai examines the factors that led to the annexation of East Jerusalem (entry 506), and the essays by Maguire (entry 495) and Tibawi (entry 502) criticize Israeli attempts to change the character of the city. Cattan's volume develops strong legal arguments against Israeli actions in Jerusalem (entry 486), while Blum defends Israel's legal claims to the entire city (entry 483). Benvenisti (entry 480), Cohen (entry 488) and Syrkin (entry 501) all contend that at least some of the Arab inhabitants' aspirations and all of their religious freedoms have and can be secured within the framework of Israeli sovereignty over the whole city. The monograph by Lord Caradon reviews several solutions to the problem (entry 485), and Wilson (entry 505) calls for the internationalization of the city, a provision that had been included in the U.N. partition resolution of 1947.

In 1984, some of Israel's staunchest allies in Congress backed a resolution calling for the transfer of the American embassy in Israel from Tel Aviv to Jerusalem (entries 503 and 504). This initiative failed due to strong opposition by the Reagan administration.

476   Aamiry, M. A. *Jerusalem: Arab Origin and Heritage*. New York: Longman, 1983.

477   Adler, Stephen. "The United States and the Jerusalem Issue." *Middle East Review* 17 (Summer 1985), 45-53.

478   Benvenisti, Meron. "Dialogue of Action in Jerusalem." *Jerusalem Quarterly*, No. 19 (Spring 1981), 10-22.

479   _____. *Jerusalem: The Torn City* . Minneapolis: University of Minnesota Press, 1976.

480   _____. "Some Guidelines for Positive Thinking on Jerusalem." *Middle East Review* 13 (Spring-Summer 1981), 35-40.

481   Berry, J. "The Jerusalem Question: Cutting the Gordian Knot." *Parameters: Journal of the US Army War College* 10 (June 1980), 33-43.

482   Bin Talal, Crown Prince Hassan. *A Study on Jerusalem*. New York: Longman, 1983.

483   Blum, Yehuda Zvi. *The Juridical Status of Jerusalem*. Jerusalem: The Hebrew University of Jerusalem, the Leonard Davis Institute for International Relations.   Jerusalem Papers on Peace Problems, No. 2, February 1974.

484   Brecher, Michael. "Jerusalem: Israel's Political Decisions, 1947-1977." *Middle East Journal* 32 (Winter 1978), 13-34.

485 Caradon, Lord (Sir Hugh Foot). *The Future of Jerusalem: A Review of Proposals for the Future of the City.* Washington, D.C.: Research Directorate, National Defense University, 1980.

486 Cattan, Henry. *Jerusalem.* New York: St. Martin's, 1981.

487 _____. "The Status of Jerusalem Under International Law and United Nations Resolutions." *Journal of Palestine Studies* 10 (Spring 1981), 3-15.

488 Cohen, Saul B. *Jerusalem—Bridging the Four Walls: A Geopolitical Perspective.* New York: Herzl Press, 1977.

489 _____. "Jerusalem's Unity and West Bank Autonomy—Paired Principles." *Middle East Review* 13 (Spring-Summer 1981), 27-34.

490 Dakkak, Ibrahim. "Jerusalem's Via Dolorosa." *Journal of Palestine Studies* 11 (Autumn 1981), 136-149.

491 Ferrari, Silvio. "The Vatican, Israel and the Jerusalem Question (1943-1984)." *Middle East Journal* 39 (Spring 1985), 316-331.

492 Kletter, L. "The Sovereignty of Jerusalem in International Law." *Columbia Journal of Transnational Law* 20:2 (1981), 319-363.

493 Kollek, Teddy. "Jerusalem: Present and Future." *Foreign Affairs* 59 (Summer 1981), 1041-1049.

494 Kraemer, Joel L., ed. *Jerusalem: Problems and Prospects.* New York: Praeger, 1980.

495 Maguire, Kale. *The Israelisation of Jerusalem.* London: Arab Research Centre, 1981.

496 Mattar, Ibrahim. "From Palestinian to Israeli: Jerusalem 1948-1982." *Journal of Palestine Studies* 14 (Summer 1983), 57-63.

497 Prittie, Terrence C. "City of Peace?" *Middle East Review* 13 (Spring-Summer 1981), 20-26.

498 _____. *Whose Jerusalem?* London: Frederick Muller, 1981.

499 Romann, Michael. "Jews and Arabs in Jerusalem." *Jerusalem Quarterly*, No. 19 (Spring 1981), 23-46.

500 Schmelz, U. O. "Notes on the Demography of Jews, Muslims and Christians in Jerusalem." *Middle East Review* 13 (Spring-Summer 1981), 62-68.

501 Syrkin, Marie. "Jerusalem Belongs to Israel: The Very Heart of the Jewish State." *Middle East Review* 13 (Spring-Summer 1981), 9-19.

502 Tibawi, A. "Special Report: The Destruction of an Islamic Heritage in Jerusalem." *Arab Studies Quarterly* 2:2 (1980), 180-189.

503 U.S. Congress. House.   Committee on Foreign Affairs. *Legislation Calling for a Move of the U.S. Embassy in Israel to Jerusalem.* Hearings and Markup, Subcommittee on Europe and the Middle East and Subcommittee on International Operations, April 10-October 2, 1984. Washington, D.C.: 1984.

504 _____. Senate. Committee on Foreign Relations. *American Embassy in Israel.* Hearing on S. 2031, February 23, 1984. Washington, D.C.: 1984.

505 Wilson, Evan M. "The Question of Jerusalem." *American-Arab Affairs,*No. 1 (Summer 1982), 111-119.

506 Yishai, Yael. "Israeli Annexation of East Jerusalem and the Golan Heights: Factors and Processes." *Middle Eastern Studies* 21 (January 1985), 45-60.

Resolving the Arab-Israeli Conflict:

Procedural Proposals

The U.S. has refused to negotiate with the PLO because it has not disavowed terrorism and has yet to accept U.N. Security Council resolution 242 which acknowledges the right of all Middle East states to live in peace within secured and recognized boundaries. Successive Israeli governments have vowed never to accept the PLO as a negotiating partner due to its commitment to destroy the Jewish state.

Alpher (entry 507), Bahbah (entry 508), Kelman (entry 511), Neumann (entry 513) and Orfalea (entry 514) lament the absence of the PLO from the peace process and recommend the initiation of direct contacts between the PLO, Israel, and the United States. On the other hand, Menahem Milson, who served as Israel's civilian administrator of the West Bank, argues that the PLO must be deprived of its political base among the Palestinians and replaced with other Palestinians more willing to cooperate with Israel (entry 512). Crown Prince Hassan of Jordan favors resumption of the peace process under the framework of an international conference in Geneva (entry 509).

507 Alpher, Joseph. "Why Begin Should Invite Arafat to Jerusalem." *Foreign Affairs* 60 (Summer 1982), 1110-1123.

508 Bahbah, Bishara. "U.S. Policy: From Straitjacket to Impasse: Why Washington Should Talk with the PLO." *Arab Perspectives* 4 (August 1983), 14-19.

509 Bin Talal, Crown Prince Hassan. "Return to Geneva." *Foreign Policy*, No. 57 (Winter 1984-85), 8-13.

510 Kelman, Herbert C. *Creating the Conditions for Israeli-Palestinian Negotiations*. Washington, D.C.:Wilson Center, International Security Studies Program, No. 25, 1981.

511 _____. "Talk with Arafat." *Foreign Policy*, No. 49 (Winter 1982-83), 119-139.

512 Milson, Menahem. "How to Make Peace with the Palestinians." *Commentary* 71 (May 1981), 25-35.

513 Neumann, Robert G. "Middle East: America's Next Steps." *Foreign Policy*, No. 59 (Summer 1985), 106-122.

514 Orfalea, G. "Why the U.S. Should Talk to the PLO." *Arab Perspectives* 2 (September 1981), 2-5.

515 Seeley, Talcott W. "Can the PLO Be Brought to the Negotiating Table?" *American-Arab Affairs*, No. 1 (Summer 1982), 75-80.

516 Tillman, Seth. "Peace in the Middle East and How to Get It." *International Studies Notes* 8 (June 1981), 12-20.

Substantive Proposals

Numerous substantive proposals for resolving the Arab-Israeli conflict have been advanced by various scholars in recent years. Heller (entry 528), Khalidi (entry 531) and Weiler (entry 543) favor the establishment of an independent Palestinian state on the West Bank and Gaza and the conclusion of a peace treaty between Israel, the new Palestinian entity, and Israel's Arab neighbors. The studies by Bull (entry 523) and Tuma and Darin-Drabkin (entry 542) conclude that an independent Palestinian state encompassing the West Bank and Gaza would be an economically viable entity. None of these studies, however, attempt to determine whether the preferred outcome is politically feasible.

The "Allon Plan," formulated by the late Israeli Foreign Minister Yigal Allon (entry 518), suggested a territorial compromise under which Israel would retain the Jordan Valley rift and the easternmost ridge of the Samarian and Judaean mountains, while permitting the Arab-populated central core of the West Bank to be politically unified with Jordan.

Arguments against the creation of a Palestinian state and in favor of the resettlement of the Palestinian refugees inside Jordan are advanced by Kampf (entry 530). Brown, however, rejects this solution and challenges the contention that Jordan should become the home for the Palestinians (entry 522).

The collection edited by El-Asmar, et al. contains several essays by those who support the partition of Palestine and those favoring a united, socialist, Palestinian-Jewish state west of the Jordan river (entry 524). At the other extreme, Rabbi Meir Kahane, the American-born founder of the Jewish Defense League and currently a member of the Israeli Knesset, argues that all Arabs must be driven out from Israel and the occupied areas in order to secure Israel's survival as a purely Jewish state (entry 529).

517 *A Compassionate Peace: A Future for the Middle East.* A Report Prepared for the American Friends Service Committee. New York: Hill & Wang, 1982.

518 Allon, Yigal. "Israel: The Case for Defensible Borders." *Foreign Affairs* 55 (October 1976), 38-53.

519   Ayoob, M. "Defusing the Middle East Time-Bomb: A State for the Palestinians." *World Today* 37 (September 1981), 323-331.

520   Ben-Yishay, Ron. "Israel's Move." *Foreign Policy*, No. 42 (Spring 1981), 43-57.

521   Bin Talal, Crown Prince Hassan. *Search for Peace*. New York: St. Martin's, 1984.

522   Brown, L. Dean. *The Land of Palestine: West Bank Not East Bank*. Washington, D.C.: Middle East Institute, Problem Paper No. 23, 1983.

523   Bull, Vivian A. *The West Bank—Is It Viable?* Lexington, MA: D.C. Heath, 1975.

524   El-Asmar, Fouzi, Uri Davis, and Naim Khadr, eds. *Toward a Debate on Palestine*. London: Ithaca Press, 1981.

525   Elazar, Daniel J., ed. *Self-Rule, Shared Rule: Federal Solutions to the Middle East Conflict*. Tel Aviv: Turtledove, 1979.

526   Feldman, Shai. "Peacemaking in the Middle East: The Next Step." *Foreign Affairs* 59 (Spring 1981), 756-780.

527   Hareven, Alouf, ed. *Is There a Solution to the Palestine Problem? Israeli Positions*. Jerusalem: Van Leer Institute, 1982.

528   Heller, Mark A. *A Palestinian State: The Implications for Israel*. Cambridge, MA: Harvard University Press, 1983.

529   Kahane, Rabbi Meir. *They Must Go*. New York: Grosset and Dunlap, 1981.

530   Kampf, Herbert. "The Real Palestinian Arab Problem." *Midstream* 28 (March 1982), 9-14.

531   Khalidi, Walid. "Thinking the Unthinkable: A Sovereign Palestinian State." *Foreign Affairs* 56 (July 1978), 695-713.

532   Klutznick, Philip M.   "Peace Need Not Only Be for Dreamers."
American-Arab Affairs, No. 8 (Spring 1984), 41-53.

533   Nakhleh, Emile A., ed.   *A Palestinian Agenda for the West Bank and Gaza.* Washington, D.C.: American Enterprise Institute, 1980.

534   Perlmutter, Amos.   "A Palestinian Entity?"   *International Security* 5, No. 4 (1981), 103-116.

535   Plascov, Avi.   *A Palestinian State? Examining the Alternatives.* Adelphi Papers, No. 163. London: International Institute for Strategic Studies, 1981.

536   Rabbo, S.   "The Palestinian Question: The Necessity of a Comprehensive Solution."   *Search* 2 (January 1981), 348-359.

537   Ramati, Yohanan.   "The 'Jordanian Option'."   *Midstream* 27 (January 1981), 8-11.

538   Rosenbaum, Aaron D.   "Discard Conventional Wisdom." *Foreign Policy*, No. 49 (Winter 1982-83), 154-167.

539   Shalev, Aryeh.   "Autonomy: Problems and Possible Solutions." *Jerusalem Quarterly*, No. 15 (Spring 1980), 3-15.

540   Steinberg, Gerald M.   "The Serbian Scenario: A Preview of the Impact of a Palestinian State on Israeli Security?"   *Middle East Review* 14 (Fall 1981-Winter 1981/82), 55-60.

541   *Toward Peace in the Middle East: Report of a Study Group.* Washington, D.C.: Brookings Institution, 1975.

542   Tuma, Elias, and Haim Darin-Drabkin.   *The Economic Case for Palestine.* New York: St. Martin's, 1978.

543   Weiler, Joseph H.   *Israel and the Creation of a Palestinian State.* London: Croom Helm, 1985.

544   Yariv, Aharon.   "Reflections on A Solution of the Palestinian Problem."   *Jerusalem Quarterly*, No. 23 (Spring 1982), 24-33.

Prospects for Peaceful Resolution

Assessments of future prospects for peaceful resolution of the Arab-Israeli conflict range from the guarded optimism of Cordesman (entry 550) and Eban (entry 551) to the dire prediction by Schiff that failure to attain significant progress in the search for peace will lead to a civil war in Israel (entry 562).

Based on interviews with Israeli and Palestinian leaders, the study by Mroz provides some room for hope in the finding that the vast majority of the respondents in both camps were willing to recognize their mutual rights to coexist in the region (entry 557). Likewise, Falk concludes on the basis of recent public opinion polling data that a majority of the Israeli public is now readier than ever before for compromise on the core controversies—willing to freeze settlements, to give up some settlements for a peace treaty, to approve territorial concessions, and to eschew annexation of the occupied areas (entry 552).

However, these findings should be read in conjunction with the revealing interviews that were conducted by Amos Oz (entry 558) and Walter Reich (entry 561) with West Bank Palestinians, Jewish settlers, and other Israelis. These conversations shed valuable light on the human and emotional dimensions of the Palestine controversy and suggest that Jews and Arabs are still very far away from accepting each other's claims to national self-determination in a divided Palestine.

545   Ajami, Fouad. "The Arab Road." *Foreign Policy*, No. 47 (Summer 1982), 3-25.

546   Amit, Daniel. "Strategies for Struggle, Strategies for Peace." *Journal of Palestine Studies* 12 (Spring 1983), 23-30.

547   Bin Talal, Crown Prince Hassan.   "Looking Ahead—and Swallowing Hard—in the Middle East." *American-Arab Affairs*, No. 1 (Summer 1982), 67-74.

548   Brown, William R. "The Dying Arab Nation." *Foreign Policy*, No. 54 (Spring 1984), 27-43.

549   Cooley, John K. "The War over Water." *Foreign Policy*, No. 54 (Spring 1984), 3-26.

550   Cordesman, Anthony H. "Peace in the Middle East: The Value of Small Victories." *Middle East Journal* 38 (Summer 1984), 515-520.

551   Eban, Abba. "No Choice but Activism." *Foreign Policy*, No. 57 (Winter 1984/85), 3-7.

552   Falk, Gloria H. "Israeli Public Opinion: Looking Toward a Palestinian Solution." *Middle East Journal* 39 (Summer 1985), 247-269.

553   Gavron, Daniel. *Isarel After Begin: Israel's Options in the Aftermath of the Lebanon War.* New York: Houghton Mifflin, 1984.

554   Green, S. "Camp David: Has It Become a Framework for War?" *World Policy Journal* 2:1 (1984), 155-168.

555   Jureidini, Paul A., and R. D. McLaurin. *Beyond Camp David: Emerging Alignments and Leaders in the Middle East.* New York: Syracuse University Press, 1981.

556   Lakehurst, M. "The Place of the Palestinians in an Arab-Israel Peace Settlement." *Round Table*, No. 280 (October 1980), 443-450.

557   Mroz, John E. *Beyond Security: Private Perceptions Among Arabs and Israelis.* New York: International Peace Academy, 1980.

558   Oz, Amos. *In the Land of Israel.* Translated by Maurie Goldberg-Bartura. New York: Harcourt Brace Jovanovich, 1983.

559   Pollock, D. "Jordan: Option or Optical Illusion." *Middle East Insight* 4 (March-April 1985), 19-26.

560   *Prospects for Peace in the Middle East: The View from Israel.* New York: Council on Foreign Relations, 1985.

561   Reich, Walter. *A Stranger in My House: Jews and Arabs in the West Bank.* New York: Holt, Rinehart & Winston, 1984.

562   Schiff, Zeev. "The Spectre of Civil War in Israel." *Middle East Journal* 39 (Spring 1985), 231-245.

563   Sharabi, Hisham. "Arab Policy and the Prospects for Peace." *American-Arab Affairs*, No. 1 (Summer 1982), 104-110.

564   *The Path to Peace: Arab-Israeli Peace and the United States. Report of the Study Mission to the Middle East.* Mount Kisco, NY: Seven Springs Center, 1981.

Author Index